Praise for *Busine*

Wow! *Business Evolution* is the most enjoyable book about how to grow your business I've ever read. The reason for this is the wonderful honesty of the author who tells her story from great success to bankruptcy to new success and even foiling the unwanted attention of a bruised hippo. The sheer practicality and 'doability' of the business learning she transfers to us shines through.

Janice B Gordon is an inspiration but also a great teacher who doesn't give her pupils an easy ride. If we want to grow personally and grow our businesses we have to change and ensure we are always relevant. Janice gives us the tools to do this.

This business book is the real deal on how to grow your business. It is a five star 'wow' for me which I will return to, time after time.

Tony Robinson OBE
Executive Chair/Co-Owner of BAB -
The Business Advisory Bureau Limited
Co-Founder of EnterpriseRockers.co.uk

More praise for *Business Evolution*

What I love about *Business Evolution* is the rarity and refreshing experience of not being harassed by business speak: Janice's words are simple and meaningful and support her own 'customer experience' ideals. Many of the most engaging parts of this book are centred on examples and her own experiences, and these support her teachings (and my views) about making business personal.

Janice grasps failure, learns from it and shares how to use it to grow stronger and smarter! This book shows you how to keep fresh eyes – when all is changing around you. *Business Evolution* gives you the freedom to celebrate your unique skills and key strengths and gives you renewed confidence in what you can do.

This is a belting good read and well worth every minute of your time to digest: working hard is not enough: it has to be working smart and knowing yourself and working hard. So be smart and enjoy!

Kelvin Moore
Lead Independent Director, Fibrocell Science USA
Business Strategy Consultancy UK

More praise for *Business Evolution*

Business Evolution is the essential business toolkit. There are so many lessons to be learnt from Janice's highs and lows as she shares her incredible experience and insights. The book is laden with practical exercises and examples, so not only are you learning from Janice's own journey, but you are getting practical tips too. Janice cuts through the clutter and noise with her 'Essential 4Ps', making it easy to create growth in your business. A must read for anyone wanting to gain clarity and focus on the modern day business essentials.

Vanessa Vallely
CEO & Founder of WeAreTheCity.com

Business Evolution is a straightforward practical business book for anyone starting in business and for those who are seeking business growth. This book helps you to construct the foundations of your business well to ensure that it grows from strength to strength. The author clearly has experience and knowledge which she shares through illuminating stories, theory and practice. What's great is that you can put the ideas straight into practice.

Jenny Garrett
Executive Coach & Author of *Rocking Your Role*

Business Evolution

Creating growth in a rapidly changing world

Janice B. Gordon

ISBN 978-1-497-30491-8

Cover design by Ambasa Bandele, Studioxdm
www.studioxdm.co.uk

Chapter images courtesy of kozzi.com
and Janice B Gordon

www.janicebgordon.co.uk
and www.theproblem-solver.co.uk

ACKNOWLEDGEMENTS

I am immensely grateful...

To Jennifer Manson (The Flow Writer) who nurtured me through the book writing process to help me bring my ideas to life.

To Avis Whyte for her support and thoroughness during my MBA and now this book.

To Lorraine O'Sullivan for her total support during my awakening and her continued and complete belief in me.

I would like to thank my friends, including Jenny Garrett and Kelvin Moore, who see more in me than I see in myself, and also Ambasa, my brilliant and insightful cover designer bringing concepts to life through design.

I feel so lucky and privileged that I have to make it count. I am forever grateful for all my lessons in life and believe I must use them to contribute to a better world.

I hope the ideas in this book set you on your path in creating the business you want, for the customers who want you. Thank you.

Important note

The views expressed in this book are the personal opinion of the author. Every situation is different, and not all advice can be generalised. When making decisions about the direction of your life and business you should use your own judgement as to what is appropriate for you and take specific, personalised advice.

Dedication

This book is dedicated to my family, above all
my parents, Cecil and Angela, whose sacrifice and
determination got me started on my path.

Contents

This path has one very distinct characteristic: it is not prefabricated. It doesn't already exist. The path that we're talking about is the moment-by-moment evolution of our experience, the moment-by-moment evolution of the world of phenomena, the moment-by-moment evolution of our thoughts and emotions. The path is uncharted. It comes into existence moment-by-moment and at the same time drops away behind us. When we realize that the path is the goal, there's a sense of workability. Everything that occurs in our confused mind we can regard as the path. Everything is workable.

Excerpt from *Comfortable with Uncertainty*
by Pema Chödrön

Foreword

by Lara Morgan

I am delighted to have been requested to write a foreword for Janice's book. I have no doubt that her infectious passion for the customer and for the importance of the relationship with customers being at the heart of her message will resonate and impact many.

I believes without sales you do not have a business and without customers you do not have sales. Unless a product can be intelligently communicated to the right customer - sales will not grow and repeat. It is repeat sales to satisfied customers that grow companies well. (Not selling and building a leaky bucket environment where you cannot deliver the customer promise.)

Business Evolution gets you and your business aligned to your customer's wants and needs so the business can sell them what they want and need, when they need it. You have to learn to prioritise your customer focus and through your own systems and process, evolution growth becomes scalable through process improvements to build closer relationships with your customers.

This book is for businesses wanting to grow their business by giving practical insights relevant in this rapidly changing global economy. It is clear Janice knows her stuff; I would highly recommend you to Buy it, Read it, Apply it & Evolve it!

Lara Morgan

CompanyShortcuts.com
Inspiring Entrepreneurs
Founder of Pacific Direct
Best Selling Author of *More Balls Than Most*

BUSINESS EVOLUTION

Introduction

It's not up to you how you fall. It's up to you how far you let yourself fall and how long it takes you to get back up and stand on your own two feet.

Sr. Tac Jeffrey Mitchell[1]

I am Janice B Gordon, The Problem Solver, and I successfully grow businesses. My aim is to inspire entrepreneurs, business owners and managers to realise their potential for growing their business.

Over the years of working for large companies and small business and growing my own businesses, I have distilled what I have learnt into the "Essential 4 Ps" for business growth: Personality, Purpose, Pleasure and Process; strategies and ideas that are relevant to the rapidly changing global business world. The global world has become personal; technology has allowed people to connect like never before. This book looks at the way we connect to create growth.

This book is not only for entrepreneurial business owners and managers; it has relevance for all start-ups, because it demystifies and simplifies the confusion in the mind of the entrepreneur as they look at their business.

When you set up in business you have your business plan in place and you think about how the plan is going to progress. You have real clarity and passion for what you do and you just want to get out there so customers can see how good you really are. You are "firing on all cylinders", you believe customers will absolutely love you, your product and service.

A couple of years in, your cylinders may be backfiring, you may be a bit downtrodden and a little bit confused. You have so many competing decisions to make and those decisions seem to take you further away from what you love to do.

The demands on your time in the business are not directly bringing in more customers – you're just dealing with the stuff that needs to be done around the business. That creates a lot of frustration and perhaps even unhappiness. You are not getting to do what you really want and love to do, you are not getting to where you really want and deserve to be, and you may not even be sure where that is.

Giving you clarity and focus in business

The purpose of this book is to give you clarity and focus in your business. If you are not doing what you really love to do in your business, if you are really not in flow, if you do not have enough customers, if you struggle to grow the business, if you feel stuck, if you feel something needs to change but you just do not quite know what or perhaps you don't know how, this book is for you.

If you do not know which of the competing things on your to-do list you need to do first; if you cannot find the time to get through that mountain of stuff on your desk and you cannot really see a clear path; if your tasks are never-ending; if you are unclear and unconfident about your future, this book is for you.

Your business may be ticking over but you want more for yourself and more for it. Business is not always easy but you did not go into business for an easy life. It does not have to be so hard, however. It is time to "take the bull by the horns" and move forward – you deserve it.

This book is designed to help you to see where you can make change; it is completely within your control. It is not easy doing what you do, but there is a way forward.

In 2012 there were an estimated 4.8 million businesses in the UK, which employed 23.9 million people, and had a combined turnover of £3,100 billion. Small and medium Enterprises accounted for 99.9% of all private sector businesses in the UK, 59.1% of private sector employment and 48.8% of private sector turnover in 2012.[2]

Small business is big business[3], which is why the focus of this book is on micro[4] to medium size businesses.

What I want is for your business to flow and for you to feel it is easy. As human beings we tend to complicate things. What I want to do is clear out all the clutter and noise, to put you back on your path so you regain your clarity of purpose. I want you to be focused, self-assured and confident.

When you are these things, customers feel it, and your business goes well. I'm here to get you back on your path, to get you operating as powerfully and as effectively as possible, to bring out the best you can be for you and your customers.

My start in business

I remember watching Sir John Harvey Jones on the television programme *Troubleshooter* and thinking, at a very young age, "I also want to turn around businesses".

My first business was a design consultancy selling in the USA and Europe; then after a contract in Botswana, Africa, I became an Independent Financial Adviser working for an accountancy practice advising micro to medium businesses. I studied for my MBA at the Cranfield School of Management and then worked with a customer experience innovation consultancy, acting for clients AOL, BP and

HSBC before starting up and growing my own businesses, which included an award-winning restaurant and bar.

After twenty-five years of experience working in businesses, advising businesses and starting and growing businesses, I decided to put that experience to work for others, offering mentoring and consultancy for growth to business owners who have at least a two year business history. I love making it easy for business people to do what they do best, only better!

Although this book is focused on strategies to grow successful micro to medium businesses, in my experience the fundamentals of business remain unchanged whether for large companies or small businesses, for business-to-business or business-to-consumer activities. Business is people-to-people. Business is about making connection: connecting you to your business, to your customers, to your team, to your tribe.

My focus is on micro to medium businesses because they form over 95% of businesses in the UK. Unlike larger companies that agree strategic change at board level and then rely on operations management to create the plan (it may be six months before the solution is implemented by which time the problem has moved) smaller businesses have the nimbleness to think today and act tomorrow.

In the last year I have advised businesses in the health and wellness, technology and apps, publishing, property and estate planning and care services sectors. I love the fact that the business environment is dynamic and I love working with dynamic businesses.

Chapter one

Motivating thinking into action

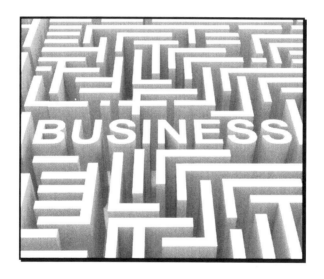

My Mission

My mission is to motivate your thinking into action. Have you ever said to yourself, "I *should* action what I have learnt. I *should* do that and I *should* make that or I *should* do it now"? If this sounds familiar, then use this book as your reference. Now is the time to take action, to turn the "I should" into "I must" and "I have".

Your thinking can change your actions. I want you to make the changes. I want you to get out your pen and paper and drill down, ask yourself the right questions until you get to the point where you feel you have the right answers. This is your time to work at changing your thinking and make a big difference to your life and business.

If you want your outcomes to be different then you need to start acting differently. This book is your starting point, your route map to find your path. You have the answers, you are unique, your customers are unique, and your business is unique. Even if you have someone next door seemingly creating exactly the same business, there will be differences; you and the characters in your business are different.

The exercises in this book are designed so you come out with the solutions, the answers that are relevant to you, your customers, your business and the people within your business.

This book is designed to guide you to find your answers. You need to do the work, you need to be committed to invest the thinking time, to sleep on the insights, to mull it over and find the path that fits you; but it will definitely be worth it.

I will help you clear out the clutter of all those competing decisions and find clarity, so you know where you are going, so it is easy for you to decide between what is critical and important and what is not, to recognise what is taking up space and time and whether or not it should be.

If you invest the time and space to think through your answers to the questions in the exercises in this book, you can emerge confident, having created a structure to move your business forward, having created your clear path to success, to be happy in your purpose, because you really understand your position in the business. You will have clarity about why your customers come to you, what message connects you to your customers and your customers to you.

Know that you absolutely deserve to have the business you desire, to have the passion back in your business, to be absolutely in flow. When that happens you do a better job for your customers, your customers and employees are happy, you are happy on your path and your business is growing. Spend the time and be committed to follow through with the work, and the rewards will be enormous.

Finding the needle in the haystack

If business is like looking for a needle in a haystack, then my work is about magnetising the needle so all you need to do is clear a path and that needle will come to you.

My passion is talking to entrepreneurs and helping them move forward swiftly, to identify and grasp opportunities. The key is to look at your business from the customer's perspective, to have the customer's experience and journey in mind as you review your business.

The core of this book is the Essential 4 Ps

Firstly, P is for Personality. Put your Personality into your business so your ideal customers can find you and engage with you, so they can be magnetised and attracted to you and the business.

Secondly, P is for Purpose. Tell your story around your Purpose, the focus of your business. Distil your story until you have a key phrase that meets the needs of your customer.

If you are a health professional, you might be in the business of pain relief. The reason customers will come to you is because they want relief from pain, so the focus of your business is pain relief. You are not in the business of a chiropractor or physiotherapist, you are in the business of pain relief. Purpose is about being focused on your core goal/objective/aim, and ensuring everything else is aligned to it.

Thirdly, P is for Pleasure, understanding the pleasure principle — as humans we are attracted to pleasure and we avoid pain. We need to speak to our customers' pleasures, their desires, their wants because this energises and motivates them.

You want to get your customers to say, "That's it, I want one of those, that's what I have been looking for, I have got to have that now". The way you can get your customer to say yes is to get them to identify themselves with your business and you with them. You need to be absolutely in tune with what their wants are.

You are servicing customers' needs so you need to understand what their problem is and provide the solution to solve their problem. For example, if you are a weight-loss company you might choose to say, "I can help you lose weight" or you might choose to say, "I can help you look great in jeans". Which of your claims best motivates the customer's desire? As a customer, I want to look great in jeans. I do not want to have a feeling of lack about my weight problem; this is painful. I know I need to lose weight but what I really want is to look great in jeans. I want to believe that the thing I desire and aspire to is possible; this is motivating and pleasurable.

Finally, P is for Process — process is about aligning to your customers' desires so that they get what they want, when they want it and how they want it.

Process is not about serving the customer's every whim; it is about making sure that you remove any barriers to your customers doing business with you, you make it easy for them to fulfil their desires. If your customers find it effortless to do business with you, why would they go anywhere else? Sometimes as entrepreneurs we make things complicated. We design processes from our own perspective. In the Process chapter we will talk about designing processes from the customer's perspective. We will go on the customer's journey and understand the problems that they have in transacting business with you. Then you can remove these blocks.

Call centres are a great example of common blocks to doing business. It is rare that you ring a call centre and they resolve the problems for you swiftly and easily. Instead you may put down the phone feeling frustrated and stressed because you were kept on hold, told you would get a call back, asked to call back with more information and so on – these are blocks in the process of the customer getting what they want and need.

We get used to all of these blocks in business. We are subjected to them all the time and we do not look on them as blocks because we think, "This is just the way life is"; but just because many people are used to having to deal with these blocks in business doesn't mean that you have to be satisfied with your business being the same.

So those are the four essential 'P's: Personality, Purpose, Pleasure and Process. If you align all the 'P's you are ready to start the journey along your growth path.

Chapter two

My Journey - Waking up the hard way

Sometimes, once we have followed our path for a while —
we have acquired the qualifications, the experience and
everything else we think we might need — we think we
have got it nailed. We are quite happy ambling along but
then something happens to knock us off the perch.

This happened to me when I was in business. I call it my awakening. My partner and I had spent over £200,000 taking the shell of a space — no windows, just four corners of walls — and turning it into a beautiful, stylish restaurant and bar. We developed it through difficult economic times into a thriving business.

It was hard work, but I loved it. Then one day I turned up for work as normal and found the landlord had changed the locks, issued a default notice under dubious pretext and let the premises to a new tenant. Everything – all the equipment and assets, even the weekend's takings and my personal items – were locked inside.

A spiralling chain of events followed, everything was completely out of control and it ended in personal bankruptcy. It was like dominoes, where one goes and you try to madly rush around and keep the others up. You are in denial and in shock but your instinct is to try and keep all of these dominoes standing. But in the end you get to a stage when you just have to let it all fall, to the stage of, "what will be, will be". You sink a bit lower and let it happen because there is no way you can control any of it.

In retrospect, this was my epiphany, an event from which I learnt a great deal; but it was also like a death, with the accompanying process of grief. It was like being in the middle of the storm, with an eerie calm around me.

I was angry about the betrayal and the deceit, re-living four years' worth of conversations, with everything anyone had ever said to me about the business perpetually going around inside me. I was trying to understand what part I had played in the story, where it all started, where I could find the seed. There are no answers in this sort of situation; nevertheless your brain continually tries to seek them.

Grief happens in stages: denial, bargaining, anger, depression and eventually acceptance. While I was in the bargaining stage it was like a record of lived events was playing eternally, until I got completely sick of it — I got sick of myself, sick of that voice and I wanted it to stop.

It was then that I made the decision that this was not going to define me; that this was not going to be my story, that this was not where it was all going to end. This was not going to be the cloak I wore for the rest of my life. This was my awakening.

I believe everything truly does happen for a reason. Emotionally, I had to deal with the fallout of bankruptcy and reconcile everything in my heart, but once I had made that decision it enabled me to very quickly move on. It is so important to take control and make decisions in life. It is your life. It is your choice.

Be careful what you wish for

Your life is about taking responsibility for everything within it. To reach this realisation is, without doubt, enlightening. I loved being in business but found the partnership stressful. There were aspects of the business, and the partnership, that I wanted to get away from. So I have to take responsibility for the consequences I attracted to me. My thoughts were negative, "I do not want this, I do not want to be in this situation, it is really difficult and I want to get out"; so I magnetised negativity.

I got out of the partnership, not in the way I thought, or would choose consciously, but it happened. Although other people took advantage of the opportunity, I allowed this opportunity; at some level I brought all of this on myself. The situation was not how I would have chosen it to be. However, once I took responsibility, I was relieved. My internal conversation morphed: "Okay, fair enough. I cannot change it, it has happened. I am responsible for my thoughts." Once you have taken responsibility there is nothing else left; the record stops playing and you get off the track.

When I was younger I found it difficult to admit to my failings, to admit that I was wrong, to take responsibility; but now it is a relief not to be perfect — so what? Now I am accepting of being wrong or admitting failings because doing so draws a line underneath negative experiences; the emotion attached to the experience is no longer important and I can let it go.

I am forever happy and grateful for the lessons that I have learnt and the beauty is, if I can attract negative things to me, I can also attract positive things. I can choose what I attract to me — that was the amazing part of the epiphany. I can choose what I want to attract into my life — that is the enlightening message. And you can attract what you want into your life, too.

This experience has made me more driven, more empowered, because I know I have the ability to attract anything I want, all the *positive* things I want; and now I want to get out there and do it.

I now understand humility. I knew what it was before but I did not fully understand it, what it meant and what it felt like. I am happier, more self-assured, more inspired to contribute and more energised. Life is the totality of the experience, not the experience itself and I am so grateful for the lesson.

I understand that I can choose to create my own happiness. I have found a path. The totality of my experience — my work in Africa, the sales training as an IFA, the fact that I can talk to anyone, my design business working in the US and Europe, my hospitality business experience and my travel adventures — the totality of my experience has taught me crucial lessons in life and business. And those lessons started with, "you choose your path".

Back to my mission

This book will help you to motivate your thinking into action to solve the problems you are facing and to bring you clarity and focus. Do not just look at your business; really see. Do not just hear; really listen.

Lessons I Have Learnt

The following are some of the most useful lessons I have learnt through all my experience. I'll list them here in the hope that you can benefit from them, too.

Lesson 1. Big Head

You may associate these words with boasting but is this association about perspective or mind talk?

Things are so much bigger in your own head. You are in a situation and it's like a roundabout, you are re-living the conversations and re-playing all the options and scenarios; you are stressed. You are worried and thinking about things that may never happen. You prepare yourself and you gird your loins for the worst.

Do you identify with this? It is so much bigger in your head and you really need to get it out of your head. How often do the predictions that you make in your head actually materialise and become a reality? Maybe forty percent of the time? Maybe only ten? Yet you spend all of that energy building yourself up for all these things that may never happen. It is a waste of your time and energy.

So get it out of your head and into the open. When you say it out loud or write down the conversation going on in your head, if you are really honest you realise the ridiculousness of it. You can question and dispel your illogical and emotional thoughts, you can dispel the stress and the worry; you realise how ridiculous you are being and you can laugh at it.

The antidote to "big head" is focusing on the "here and now". Do not let your brain race into the future in thinking about all of these scenarios: be present.

Sports professionals use various triggers to anchor the feeling of success. When they win they may shout "yes!" They might pump their arm in the air or look up to the sky, stamp their feet, do the "Mobot" or the "Bolt". You can do the same.

Whatever you do as your anchor, follow it with a positive affirmation like, "I choose happiness" or "this is it". This brings you back to your here and now and your path. If you are the type of person who constantly races ahead and loses control of your thoughts, just stamp your feet, here and now and bring yourself back down to earth.

Lesson 2. Where is it?

Ask yourself:

"Is it in the past?" If you're thinking about something that is in the past, something that is already done, you cannot change it. It is already gone; money already spent. It is done. Leave it alone, it is history so put it away.

"Can you change it?" If it is something you can have an impact on then change it and change it now. Get it out of your head and act on it right away. Pick up the phone, speak to that person and clear your mind. It is cluttering up your head and taking a lot of energy. If you cannot change it, it is in the past. So leave it alone.

"Is it in the future?" If it is something in the future, then why are you thinking about it now? Why is it taking up valuable space in your head? There is nothing you can do about it yet, so leave it alone for now. Come back into the here and now.

Once you have gone through these three questions, the other antithesis to Big Head is gratitude. Every day I am grateful and that keeps me energised, reminding me why I am here, what I am meant to do. I think about the people around me and the journey that I have been on. It is so easy to wallow and to remain stuck. We often put ourselves in that position — and it is comfortable — it is not attractive, but it is easy.

Sometimes we need to enjoy wallowing and give ourselves a little bit of space to mourn. But set yourself a time limit: an hour to cry, scream or moan to your best friend; one day to wrap yourself up in a blanket, sit on the sofa and wallow. After that time, that's it, it is done. Remind yourself you are not here just to wallow, there is more to your story, so it is time to get out of your head and move on.

Lesson 3. What are you waiting for?

Sometimes we demand perfection. We like to get it all sorted in our heads and make it all perfect and have every step of the big idea, of whatever we are doing, absolutely nailed before we move off.

If you want to get from 'A' to 'B', you generally plan out the route but when we are talking about ideas in business, about getting started or doing something you have never done before, sometimes you need to discover by doing. Just get moving.

If you knew all the steps you probably would not do it, because what's the point? Taking action is a voyage into the unknown, a path of discovery. Recognise business is dynamic and life is not perfect. There is no perfect plan so do not get paralysed by fear of the unknown – doing is learning and learning is knowing.

I see entrepreneurs who are in their own head obsessing over something that is not important to their customer, for example, spending fortunes on perfect websites before thoroughly tested their idea; it is important to allow that idea to evolve over time and with experience. The website evolves along with the idea, the customer and the business.

Lesson 4. Leave your past baggage behind

Have you noticed the more baggage you carry the heavier the load? Everything happens for a reason but if you are clogged up with all of your past experiences you are not going to live your current experiences with an open heart, with the expectation of and room for new things to come to you. There is too much already in there obstructing your perceptions. Clear out the clutter, put the baggage down, and move on.

Lesson 5. Focus on the goal

Have a clear vision of the future. It is important to be really focused on the goal ahead. Focus on your path, not the path of others. Look ahead in the direction you are travelling, so you can see the opportunities and the gifts that will help you achieve your goal. Ask, "will this help me to achieve my purpose?" This will help you to remain on your path and in flow.

Lesson 6. Play to your strengths

Play to your strengths and hire great people to cover your weaknesses. As much as it is nice to know everything, it is not possible to master it all. Life is too short to be good at everything.

What is wonderful is you only have to be great at one thing and that is being the best you can be. You are here and you are great at some things, celebrate your greatness and do not try to do the things you are not great at — get other great people in. Initially in business you may have to do everything yourself but as soon as you can, get to a point of bringing in people with complementary skills; you will be able to do more of what you are great at and scale your business faster.

Playing to your strengths is like swimming with the current and not against it. Moving forward faster is a case of going with your energy and not against it.

Lesson 7. Integrity

One important thing I have learnt is about integrity, being really true to myself. One of my mantras is, "If I am not feeling it, I am not doing it". I do not want to do things in a resentful way, or because I feel I have to. I want to do things with an open heart, being 100% present and engaged; it is better for me and others.

It may be "no" for now, I may do it in the future. It may just be that I am focused on a particular goal and need to get that done first; so if I am not feeling it I am not doing it and that is fine. It's OK to say "no".

I want to do everything 100% present, engaged and openhearted. When I do this, I am going to do it effortlessly and to the best of my abilities.

My top value

The most important thing to me is being in my flow, using my positive energy to do what I do best. This helps me to stay focused on my path and to move forward with certainty.

Having a mentor

We all need mentors. Sports personalities all have coaches and mentors to make the difference to get them on to the next stage. Business people are no different. If we knew how to get there we would all be there already. If you want to get where you are going faster, it helps to ask someone who has a different perspective, more knowledge and/or experience, for directions. Find someone who has the next piece of the puzzle that you need to fit into your path, so that you can move on to the next stage.

It is really important to find someone you can connect with, who engages you. Be clear about what you want and need to help you achieve your purpose.

How a business mentor can help

I have had several mentors and advisors in my business and life. I believe we can learn a great deal from the experience of others. Mentors have supported me through difficult decisions, given me access to other networks and contacts and introduced me to new ways of thinking and strategies which I have applied to my business. We cannot know it all and we need to continually develop ourselves to grow ourselves. A mentor can be the equivalent of reading a lifetime of experience.

You may need clarity of purpose or help developing strategies to get you there. To get to where you want to go you need to be motivated and committed to change with continuous personal growth and development. A business mentor can help you to get on your path and keep you motivated to stay on it.

You may be thinking about structure, strategy and growth, how to best expand your business, how to develop new markets or how to market effectively to new and existing customers; in all these areas a business mentor can support you.

Dreaming big

The dream for your business has got to be so big that it is scary. It has got to be so big that you don't have all the pieces to make sense of the jig-saw; you will identify the gaps and learn the skills you need as you journey along your path. This is why working with a mentor grows your business faster. A mentor helps you to find the pieces that fill those gaps. It is not necessary for you to have all the pieces from the "get go". You only need the pieces to move your business from 'A' to 'B' but when you are moving to 'C' and there are some missing pieces of knowledge in your business jig-saw you go out and get that information when you need it.

Do not be afraid of having your vision so big that it is going to take you to 'Z'. That is fine, you will get there. Do not have a dream that is only a 'C' dream, just because you do not know how you are going to get to 'Z'. If you do that you are not really fulfilling your dream, you are playing safe. If you want to play safe get a salary.

As an entrepreneur in business you have got to be comfortable with being uncomfortable. The point is not to have all the pieces of the jig-saw; the point is to trust that you can get the missing piece when you need it.

Mentoring really helps, with clarity and focus, with getting on with fears and fulfilling your big dream. Mentors help you be comfortable with being uncomfortable, to feel deeply self-assured.

Your business is all about the customer

Your business is not about you; it is all about the customer. Without customers you have no business so your business and your marketing activities need to be absolutely focused on your customer, their journey, their experience, what you can do to solve their problem. If your business is completely attuned to your customer and if you have the customer's head in your business then you are going to excel way over and above what the competition is doing – because so few businesses do this well. This is the marketing that makes the difference. In this book you will learn to align your business personality, your purpose and your processes to your customers' pleasure.

What the journey of this book is going to be like for you

Your job is to be an active driver as you journey through this book. I am really passionate about motivating you to change your thinking, which in turn changes your actions and your destiny.

When there is change it is natural that you go through a bit of resistance. You may have doubts, such as, "What is the point in this?" or, "This is not going to work or make any difference for me". Try to push through doubt and just go with the flow. You may not always understand why you are doing things but it is a journey and when you are on a journey, sometimes it is nice just to look at the scenery, not judge it and not set any expectations but just follow the road.

Do it with an open heart and an open mind because you do not know everything; once you come out at the other end and you can look back and you see the progress that you have made, then you can see the learning. You cannot always see the learning at the beginning of the process, it's at the end when you can look back and reflect that it becomes clear. Sometimes you just need to go with it, just trust in the process. After all, this is what we are asking our customers to do isn't it? We are asking them to have a little bit of faith, trust in the process and go with it. We're asking them to exchange money to try our product or service.

Just trust in the process. The important thing is to keep going, to keep working through the exercises. You do not always know what you need until you need it.

There will come a time when you turn on that motor, tap into that thing that focuses you, that energy point that moves you forward.

The more you put in, the more you will get out. We know this in life; I absolutely know this is true in business. Life is not meant to be a bed of roses. We learn when things are challenging, that's the point of why we are here. Expect some bumps in the road. Expect road closures and diversions along the way. When they happen, pick up the challenge, ride the bumps, take the diversions, see what you can learn from them.

This book is about finding your path so you can achieve your goal of growing your business and thus being happy in your flow. Let me help you find your path, let me help you navigate your path because this is your life, this is your business and this is Business Evolution.

This book is about you, your business, and your customers. If you are aligned with your business, then you are in flow and your business is in flow; if you and the business are aligned with your customers, then your customers are in flow with your business. This is **Business Evolution**.

In this book I will share my insights and ideas – and, I hope, motivate you to take action. The rest is up to you.

Welcome to Business Evolution!

Chapter three

Personality

Today you are You, that is truer than true. There is no alive who is You-er than You. [5]

Dr Seuss

What is your Personal Business Personality?

Putting your personality into your business allows customers to identify and engage with you and your business. It is important to have unique characteristics in your business that customers can identify with.

The one thing we all know very well is our own personality and character. Part of the process of growing your business is learning to love what you are and what you have; your uniqueness is what distinguishes you. If you do not love who you are, how do you expect others to like you, to trust you and what you stand for, to trust your values and your business?

It is so important to tell customers who you are, what you are about and just be proud of being YOU; there is no one "You-er". Customers will get your values and personality quicker and trust you because it is the real you, it is your unique view. Customers love the honesty.

Case Study: Liz

I began my meeting with a prospective client, a secretarial virtual assistant who I will call Liz, by assessing her website. From Liz's body language I could tell immediately that she was not confident about her website. The site looked like something for a therapy business. It had an aqua, calming look-and-feel to it. Liz's website did not reflect her.

When I met Liz she was wearing canary yellow – not a colour that would be worn by those lacking in confidence!

She looked vital and vibrant, she was effervescent with energy, totally different from her website. Liz's site was trying to be something that she was not. Although she speaks calmly and is a very methodical, well-planned and well-organised person, Liz has a luminescent and joyful personality that was not captured by her sedate and languid website. Her true personality and the personality of the business did not match up.

When there is a disconnect between what you say and what you do, other people do not buy into it – yet that's exactly what you want your customers to do, to get you and to buy you. What are you about? What is your story? What do you do? Your message needs to be clear and consistent. Customers identify with the values they see in you and your business; values that they also see in themselves. When we look in the mirror we do not see our true self, we see a reflection of our perception of our self.

For example I look in the mirror and see myself as two sizes larger than I am. My reflection shows me size 12 but my brain tells me I am size 14 or 16 depending on my emotional state and that is what I see. My perception of myself is larger.

Having talked it through, Liz decided to make some changes. She felt such relief in taking off the cloak of her perception of what she thought was professional and acceptable. Liz had thought she needed to create this rather staid image to be taken seriously in business. She did not have a picture of herself on her website, in fact there was very little of Liz there at all.

We spend a lot of energy trying to fill all the gaps that are not true to who we are. Once Liz saw this and was confident enough to get rid of that cloak and just let customers see her for who she is — bold and talented — she became clear about her skill to help other businesses and she was able to let go of the false persona and put her energy into being the best of herself.

We revised the website to reflect Liz's true self. I gave Liz a new perspective on how her customers interpret her communication, which enabled Liz to communicate in the language of the customer and market to those people who had a need for her skill.

Liz's skills had not changed at all but now that customers could see her true self they could trust her and recommend her. Existing customers felt more comfortable with the image and potential customers loved the revised site and the relaxed Liz.

When I saw Liz two months later she was smiling, so much more relaxed. She said, "Everything has changed for the better in my business." In fact it was Liz who had changed, not her customers or her business. Her true personality and confidence were coming out. She is no longer spending all her energy keeping this false cloak of perceived professionalism and distance in place. Business is happening a lot more easily for Liz, because Liz is in her flow.

We all absolutely love meeting someone who is full of character. It is a privilege to get a little insight into their soul, into what makes them "Them". It is an honour when someone trusts you enough to let down their guard and share with us a little bit of themselves. This is true connection. We feel privileged when someone allows that to happen; it is lovely having an exchange that shares real value. That is what we want in business: for customers to feel comfortable because they are getting the real personality.

Movements in the global economy

I relish and embrace the way the global economy is moving. Even connecting business to business is about connecting people to people; business is moving away from "who you know" toward "what you stand for and who you are". People want to know you because of what you have to share. This is the way the business world is changing, the global world has become personal, technology allows people to connect; this book looks at the way we connect with others to create growth. This is Business Evolution.

I am extremely excited about the future. I see change as an opportunity. Opportunities are not easy to catch, however. You have to be willing to embrace change and change is uncomfortable. I often say, "To be in business is to be comfortable with being uncomfortable". We are in a rapidly changing world and business must embrace change.

Business has to cope with the speed the Internet makes possible. Technology is mobile, enabling business to be transacted anywhere in the world and at any time, with mobile payments commonplace. Today's customers are powerful. They are the drivers of crowd-sourcing of everything and anything. Customers have the power to shop globally from their bedroom, indeed global is now local and cross collaboration is becoming easy.

The latest revolution in production is 3D printing: don't make it, print it! How can all this affect your business? How can you take advantage of change?

Change is rapid. We are moving from trading on position to trading on personality and this includes your business, or the company you work for. When we think of Apple we think of Steve Jobs, when we think of Virgin we think of Richard Branson. The business is synonymous with the business personality.

Your business personality is about getting people to identify and engage with you and your business – this is why introducing your personality into your business is so important in the social global economy. I am not talking about giving people personal information; do not get caught up in paranoia. I'm talking about the type of things that you would share with an interviewer if you were selling your skills and your values. I'm talking about your experiences in business and in life that add up to who you are as a character. A character in a play would not be one dimensional and neither are you. This is the personality you need to put into your business; your "You-ness".

People buy from people

People buy people. There is a saying, "It's just business, it's nothing personal", or as Michael Corleone (Al Pacino) put it in the Godfather, "It's not personal, Sonny, it's strictly business". I absolutely disagree with this. Business is all about the personal; it is about building trust, and you do not build trust with inanimate objects, you build trust with people. Unless you have that rapport and trust you are not going to transact business very successfully or for very long.

This is why large businesses commit time and money to building a brand, a personality in which the customer can place trust. Nowadays much of business is not done face-to-face, so it is all the more important to put your personality into your business. It is almost like a mirror reflection of yourself – it is some of you but not all of you – enough to give a brand identity that customers can engage with; because people do absolutely buy people. They get a sense of trust from your values, your voice, your character, your vision. Unless they identify with these things, with your true personality, then customers are not going to trust and buy your product, your service and you.

Building loyalty

Customers will often test the waters first by making a small purchase. Then if it works out well they will go back and look at the communication around what they have purchased: perhaps they will purchase something bigger. With the experience, they will become loyal to you. Customers won't shop around because of the positive connection and experience they have from you. That's how you grow business; but loyalty comes not only through the use of products and services, it comes through the personality, the values and the processes. It comes through the total, consistent message and experience that your business delivers.

How to identify the parts of your personality to put into your business

First, look at what your passion is in life. Then look at your unique skills. You then need to start drilling down a bit further into the characteristics: what is your experience, what are your values, what inspires you, what gives you joy, what are your key fears? Yes, even fears are important, because we all have them. Customers will engage with those as well.

What are your key lessons in life? What are the key insights that you have had that made a difference and perhaps have even taken you in a different direction? What are your key achievements? What you are looking for are your milestones, the things that caused you to stop and think, to change track or to look at the internal or external you, differently.

You are looking for the things that have taken you to where you are now, that have moulded you into the person you are now; that is what you need to pull out. The list below will help to identify the top ten characteristics that you believe will engage and connect you to your audience.

Exercise One: Identify Your Unique Key Characteristics:

Take a piece of paper and make some notes on the following: Think of your circle of friends – what are the common characteristics that bind your circle in each of these areas?

- Passions
- Unique Skills
- Values
- Look/Style
- Hobbies/Interests
- Experiences
- Fears
- Key Lessons
- Joys
- Unique Knowledge
- Mindset/Views
- Key Challenges
- Inspirations
- Family relationships
- Unusual Achievements
- Milestones
- Politics/Religion (use caution and a light touch – remember it is to connect, not disconnect).

You might ask, "Why is any of that important to my business?" It is important because it all becomes part of your story, part of telling people who you are. Once you start to pull out those things, then you will start to identify the key factors that other people can identify with.

If you are a mother with children, one of the important characteristics of your life is going to be your children. Your perspective of your world is going to be through the filter of family and children and this will influence your view and daily experiences. This will have an effect on how you run and develop your business.

People who are buying your product or service may have similar challenges because they too have children. If you start to pull this out as one of the key characteristics that you want to portray in your business, other people who identify with this key characteristic see there is a connection or synergy with their values or challenges and this customer will engage with you.

Conversely, if the customer does not share the same values or challenges as you, they may not engage with your business, or with you – but you cannot be all things to all people.

Once you put a consistent message out, people will say, "I get where you're coming from, I like your views", they can identify with your characteristics and values because they share them.

Exercise Two: Portray these characteristics in a personal statement

Once you have done your ideas exercise, drilling down and highlighting the characteristics, you need to put them into a story or statement, which you can refine until you have one powerful paragraph to use on your website, perhaps on your biography page.

Unlike a chronological CV, this paragraph or personal statement is about giving customers an essence of who you are. It forms the foundation to your business brand.

Take some time and formulate your personal statement.

You can also use your personal statement as an introduction to you and your business when making a pitch or presentation to potential customers or stakeholders. It shows others who you are. You can distil your personal statement down further until you have one sentence of up to twelve words. This sentence will allow customers to instantly get who you are and what you are about, like a personal tagline. You can use the personal statement (the large form) or the personal tagline (the short form) in your website to portray your personality.

My personal tagline is "a problem solving journey"[6], this reflects the fact of my being on my path, fluidly moving through challenges.

My business tagline is "thought-through solutions for business people" – I create bespoke solutions for people in business.[7]

Like attracts like

Imagine you are on a train and there is a group of extremely loud people, so loud that you just wish they would turn the volume down, it is hurting your ears. You do not realise it, but the group cannot hear the volume. That's a normal level for them because like attracts like. They are loud people and they speak loudly, they enjoy that level of excitement and express it with volume.

Like attracts like, so when you have a colourful personality other colourful people automatically come up and say "I love what you're wearing" or "I love what you do". They are magnetised in their attraction to you. The reason for this is they can identify with you; there is an essence of similar preferences or values. This is called the Law of Attraction.

Social psychology teaches us that similarity is a crucial determinant of interpersonal attraction. Studies about attraction indicate that we are strongly attracted to people similar to ourselves[8], so you need to reveal your personality to attract similar types of personalities or personalities that are attracted to your type of personality. What is naturally true in life is also true in business.

Drill down and look at your key characteristics. When you portray these in your business, people like you and will be attracted to do business with you. You do not have to go out there and start pulling them in; they are automatically attracted to you, just like that group of loud people on the train.

How is it that they all found one another? Why is it that the level of noise offends no one in the group? Because they cannot hear it: their attraction to one another drowns it out.

This is about using what is naturally true about you. There is no point in fighting against your nature and thinking you need to be something you are not. No, you need to be you, exactly who you are. Embrace your "You-ness", then people will automatically be attracted to you, and consequently two things result. One is that you are more attractive in business; the other is that you will attract the people you enjoy working with. Like people will find you. You do not have to find them; your personality will attract them.

Here is another example. Have you ever had a conversation with a stranger and been attracted to them (not necessarily physically) like a warm feeling of wanting to know more about why they said what they said in the way they said it? You recognise something in them and you just know you will get on. You want to know what connections or similarities you share. You realise they are like you. It is a warm and comfortable feeling and you want to learn more about them, do more with them. You cannot help yourself, you cannot fight your attraction to them.

That is exactly what you want to happen in your business with your customers. The customers attracted to you and your business will be a lot easier to work with because you are communicating in the same way. You use the same keywords, you make similar types of connections and you have a similar sense of humour. Everything flows beautifully and business is so much easier.

Business has changed

The business environment has changed enormously. It used to be very male dominated, not only in its physical form but also in its boisterous language and culture. Therapy businesses were considered as involving soft skills and were the domain of women. Male cooks were referred to as chefs, female cooks were just cooks!

Local was for regional and global was for big companies. We did not talk about engagement; we talked about sales. Connection and empathy in business were unheard of. A partnership was really a takeover, building a relationship was something you did within a marriage contract, not a business contract.

When I was growing up we had pen friends not fans or "likes", we sent letters not emails, we spoke on the telephone, we did not Skype. So much has changed: change is rapid and change is constant.

Of the businesses surveyed by Constant Contact, 49% said it is harder to keep pace with technology now than it was five years ago. Another 84% said the biggest change in how we do business now versus the last five years is the use of online marketing tools. It reported that 59% of respondents took the view that it is harder to run a business today than five years ago and 40% said there is more direct competition.[9]

Everything has changed and the rate of change is accelerating. This is having a profound effect on the way we live and the way we live is the way we transact and relate to business.

Men typically use social platforms to climb the career ladder, whereas women use them to connect and share experiences.[10] Women, in general, are very social, they find it very easy to connect and engage. The growing influence of technology on business and the need for businesses to connect digitally and amplify their message gives women (the natural connectors) an advantage in business evolution.

The masculine influence is less collaborative and more positional. Neither is wrong or right but a changing world requires a change in the way we communicate, connect, engage and transact.

The rebalancing of skills in business is giving women a real advantage in this business environment that is becoming more balanced, allowing the use of social (softer) skills to grow business. This is why creating growth in the changing world of business requires a rebalance of skill set; the way business is evolving gives this new skill set more influence than ever before.

Fear of change is quite natural. We are used to the old business systems and we are still learning the new systems, the new rules around business; and with this comes fear and doubt.

The past is spent, the future is still evolving: focus on the here and now. We need to look for the positive opportunities future businesses will create for the way we will live and interact. We need to catch the surf and ride it. To do this we need to be very much more open, more social; we need to connect, form partnerships and evolve our businesses.

A growing number of entrepreneurs are running businesses from their home and setting up businesses through social networks. There are lots of small global niche businesses. The ethos of this book is to be global, think local and act personal. Smaller businesses already have the advantage of nimbleness, they are already thinking local-global: what they need is to get their message above the parapet.

"We've gone from being exposed to about 500 ads a day back in the 1970s to as many as 5,000 a day today."[11] through TV, radio, technology, our eyes and our conversations. With so much noise, you only get a second to capture your customer's attention. You need an amplified and clear message which will grab that attention.

This is why your personality in your evolving business is so important. Business is changing. If you are setting up a business using the old marketing methods, your business is not going to survive in the future. You need to be brave and recognise these changes to capture the surf, ride it, move forward and grow. Change is happening and accelerating, businesses cannot afford not to evolve using what they have that is unique and true, and that is personality.

Maslow's hierarchy of needs

In 1943 Maslow created his hierarchy of needs, often depicted in pyramid form, which explains human motivations.[12] His ideas are keenly exploited in the field of marketing in order to understand the psychology of how people react and what their needs are.

In Maslow's hierarchy you cannot get to the top of the pyramid unless you have laid all the building blocks underneath. So, for instance, unless you have air to breathe and water to drink (the basic level building blocks), there is no point striving to get to the building blocks of friendship or love; without the basics you are not going to survive. At the very basic level, motivation is about the need for food, water, shelter and sleep.

The next level is about security and employment, so that you can meet your needs and take care of your health. At this level you have a home to go to and money coming in to pay bills; this level is about improving your quality of life.

At the highest level is self-actualisation: full expression of yourself. At this level it is important to accept things the way they are and not fight them. Self-actualisation is about morality, creativity and spontaneity and being very comfortable with being you. It is about not being threatened or prejudicial. It is being very comfortable with where you are "here and now"; being comfortable with just being.

In order to get to self-actualisation you need to achieve a level of self-esteem, of confidence in your work and your home environment. You need the respect of your society, your community and the people around you.

Once the lower levels are fulfilled, you have food and water and you have money coming in, your health, you have got somewhere to live; what is the next thing to aspire to? The next thing is connection.

You may not have a family unit, you may not have many friends, you may not have intimate relationships; the sadness that results from this can lead to poor physical and mental health. This is why social connection is important. It is so important to touch someone every day, it is so important to connect with other people. We know when we feel disconnected we do not feel happy. Before you can reach self-actualisation, you need to feel the comfort and the happiness that comes from having someone to talk to and share with.

So how does Maslow's hierarchy of needs apply to your business, to putting your personality into your business?

We used to live in social, close-knit village communities; however, with the fragmentation of traditional community there has been a loss of social connection. With the proliferation of platforms like Facebook, community can now be found online. Community is not only online it is mobile, fluid and global. What binds community? Shared values and interest. We are amalgamating the way we live, transact business and commune.

If we accept that most of our customers and the people we engage with have accomplished the first two levels of basic needs, then what we all want now is to move to a higher level and to grow in confidence in their self-expression.

Maslow's focus was looking at people's future rather than their past - their aspirations. His hierarchy helps us to understand the psychology of how people will react, transact and commune in life and in business. Maslow believed that people strive to seek their higher desires. This book is aligned to finding our own and our customers' higher desires.

This translates into business becoming more personal, more engaged and connected and social, more intimate. We are all looking for meaning: business owners, employees and customers, it is about making connections with people that you do business with. Making connection is business, and personality allows us to make those connections deeper.

Matching the connection to the customer

We hear a lot about engaging your customers, the belief that the more you engage with your customers the better it is for your business. Unfortunately, in many cases that tends to mean bombarding customers with lots of information and noise. On a higher level, however, it is more about an exchange of transforming experiences, recognition and engagement (the like attracts like response).

Some groups of customers want a lot of information on a regular basis. Some groups of customers want very little exchange: once they have bought from you and they have bought into your values, they will remain loyal. However, you must be sensitive to the way you connect and engage with any group of customers to avoid alienation.

Different customers want different types of contact: some want jokes and others want technical information. Successful connection is about connecting to the right person at the right time in the right way. It is not about "one size fits all" because personalities are different. Not only are you unique and different but your customers are, too. Making a connection to someone is about finding out what level of connection and what type of connection they want. Some people want friendship; some people want a more formal connection. Once a connection is made, engagement is ongoing and the method of that engagement is important.

Depending on your business, your products and services, this will mean different things to different people. The important thing is to connect to your customers, but I reiterate, one size does not fit all. Find out about your customers, work out what level of connection they want; then they will be happy, they will become loyal. When the communication is right for them, they engage more with you, your personality and your business.

Next, we'll start to uncover your personal passions, and how these can become part of your business. First, though, let's do a brain dump, because sometimes when we start an exercise we digress and go off track. My solution to this is to do a complete brain dump before I start.

Exercise Three: The Brain Dump

Take a piece of paper and ten minutes to write down anything that comes into your mind. Just dump it all on to that piece of paper. Don't worry about grammar or spelling or completing sentences. You will probably never look at that piece of paper again, but you need to get everything out of your head so you have clarity to answer the questions that follow.

Exercise Four: What are your Personal Passions?

In this exercise, we are going to look for your passions. Once you've done the ten-minute brain dump, sit down quietly and ask yourself: "What are my key passions"? Some people will be able to reel them off straight away, "I am passionate about school, or my children" – or whatever it may be – but sometimes your passions are buried deep. I am not saying they are not real passions but sometimes it is difficult to work out what they are; the brain dump gets all the surface information out, so that you can drill deeper.

I know I have got to my passion when I feel an emotional connection in my heart. Whenever I think about those passions, I get a warming feeling inside my gut. For some it is sweaty palms, or hair standing up at the nape of their neck. Some people might get a level of excitement or feel more emotional. Whatever your reaction, take note. It is going to be different for each person but it is important to notice it, so you can identify your emotional passion point when it happens at other times.

Continues...

Exercise Four continued...

Write down your passions and your emotional reaction to them. And not just your business passion but anything in your life that you are passionate about now.

If you are finding this difficult, ask people close to you about their perspective on what you are passionate about. You might be quite surprised what others say. Just write it down, it will become clear later. Sometimes we do not see what's obvious or what is right in front of our face. Instead, we take it all for granted or we do not take note of our emotional reactions; we operate on autopilot. We support our children in school, watch football games or we play a sport. We may not consider ourselves passionate about these things because we just do them, but these may, in fact, be the things we are most passionate about.

Exercise Five: What are your Unique Skills?

What we are after now is: "What can you do that no one else can do, in the way that you do it?" "What are your unique skills, the skills only you possess?"

Spend a bit of time working that out and again, if you are struggling with it, ask somebody close to you, this time in the work context, a close work colleague, "What do you see that I can do that no one else does or that is different in the way that I do it?" Again, you might be surprised by what others say. These things are important to recognise because that is part of your uniqueness.

How can this be used in business?

I worked with a beauty and styling client with twenty years' experience in helping others present themselves in the best light, building confidence inside and out. When I started to work with her, this question and answer exercise drew out her unique skill set, values and passions.

A few milestone experiences in her life motivated and drove her to work in a particular way, to work on the client's confidence and aspirations before making them feel and look good outside.

My client was very inspirational and her defining word (more about these later) was "inspiration". Her passion was inspiriting people. She likened this realisation of her passion to enlightenment. Once she realised that her passion was inspiring people, she felt so much happier, so much more energised. She doesn't see herself as being inspirational but she loves seeing her customers get to a point in their life where they want to share their lessons with other people, so her passion was to inspire them. Inspiring others made her work easy and excited her to do more.

Using your passions in your business

Why is passion so important? Because when you are living your passion, everything becomes easy, it is effortless. That's why sometimes it is difficult to find your passion: because it is easy and effortless, you do not see it. Just like when a footballer scores a goal and it looks so easy! Whenever anyone does something to an optimum level, it looks simple. In fact it is not simple, they have trained for it, they have honed their skill over many years, to the point where they do not even have to engage their brain; their skill flows naturally.

That is what you want in business, you want to work through your passion, the thing that is effortless for you. This doesn't mean that you do not use your skills but you combine your skills and your passion together, so that everything works effortlessly and beautifully. We are working on finding your flow in business – this is what these exercises help you to discover.

My confidence and styling client is now doing more public speaking engagements, using her unique skill as a platform to promote her passion to inspire. She is winning more business, because people can see that she is passionate about what she does – the benefits – and they engage with her. And not only are they getting her skill but in working with her they are inspired to do what they do that is great as well.

Her audience has been inspired by her courage to go out and do more and she is energised by their inspiration. It is wonderful to see her influencing people with her passion. She is not just changing someone's image and lifting their confidence, she is changing their life.

Can you imagine being able to change somebody's life? How energising would that be in your business? This is why it is important to get in touch with your passion and to look at what your unique skills are – because when you start to bring those two things together, wow, you are in your flow!

It is not easy to see what is in front of your face

When I mentor business people I can see their uniqueness straightaway. I pick up clues from what they say and how they say it; but often it is not easy for them to see their uniqueness themselves.

My role is to get you to see more of your true self.

Other people often see more in you than you see in yourself. This is especially true of women, who tend to under-rate their skills. Sometimes when we look in the mirror we do not see our real image or true self: what we see is usually shorter, fatter. We all have blind spots. Our family or friends may say, "You are brilliant at this" and we think, "Who, me"?

You may think, "They do not know me" but they absolutely know you and they see your brilliance all the time. It is just that sometimes you cannot see it for yourself.

When I work with business people, one of my roles is to get them to see what I see and get them to believe in their brilliance. I do not have those negative messages broadcasting in my head, which may be undermining their perspective of themselves.

It is a real mental block when you have a great business and you want to move it forward and you have all the potential and talent to do so but you may be talking yourself out of success and fashioning reasons why it is not going to happen.

I do not have any of this self-talk about my clients and this is why I can believe in them more than they may believe in themselves. My job is to get them to where I am in seeing themselves, set them free to go forward with absolute certainty. If you have absolute certainty your customers are going to have it, too, that absolute belief in you and your business.

Find yourself a mentor who can do this for you, help you get rid of the clutter and get you out of yourself, out of those negative messages, to see things as they are. Allow them to put a mirror up in front of you so you can see your real image. Then you will build up the courage and confidence to go out and do what you do that is great.

If you ever feel yourself slipping, if you feel the negative messages or doubts creeping back, then put that mirror in front of you again and say, "Look, this me, this is absolutely me! This is what I do that is great. This is what I believe." With a compatible mentor you speed the journey to your chosen destination.

The voices in your head can hold you back from taking bold action. Most of the time we are not conscious of the self talk but our body language is a visible sign. I see this in my clients, and then I question the communication going on in their heads. This is usually something they have not identified for themselves. From the outside it is as obvious to me as the messages on those red dot-matrix signs at train stations. You know the ones: they give you updated information on train times, boarding platforms etc. Well, that's what I see in my clients' facial expressions: I can see the doubt, I can see the lack of confidence, I can see negative body language and when they hit their emotional passion point.

I will pick up on what I see. I will question their body language and they will say, "Hang on a moment, I am feeling doubt". I can then interrogate these doubts and help my client to break down those doubts by acknowledging them and questioning the belief that underlies those feelings.

Unless someone puts a mirror up and shows you those messages they will keep circulating and keep undermining so much of what you do. You just do not need that.

Putting your story into your business

As I have said before, your story is not your chronological CV, it is about the milestones or events in your life that have made you the person you are; the things that have made you stop and think and change; the things that have made you move in a different direction, take another action or embrace a different thought or belief.

Your milestone may be a person. It may even be something negative. Our challenges can shift what we believed to be true and can motivate action to get us moving in a different direction. It could be a lesson in life that you have learnt because of an event. In the next exercise we will look at those key aspects in your life.

11111111111111111111

Exercise Six: What is your Story?

The way you get to your story is by going back over your life and recognising those key milestones and events that made you change track. The first thing to do is merely to record them on a timeline. You might want to start just listing out your skills, values, lessons, passions – these can be a good starting point.

Once you have got those down on paper, review the list and categorise it into the bigger key incidents and the lesser.

Take the four most profound events in your life that have played a large part in you being who you are and for each of them, write a few descriptive sentences.

If that is not flowing freely, try very quickly writing down your biggest skill, your biggest value, your biggest lesson, your biggest passion, your biggest fear, your biggest joy, your biggest characteristic, your biggest insight, your biggest achievement and your biggest challenge. Then add to the list with other things in each category. Then go back and categorise them and write your descriptive sentences as above.

Continues...

Exercise Six continued...

Put the list away for a few days then take it out and display it somewhere visible where you can look at it every now and then. You might start to change it, to re-write it so it flows a bit better. You might even question whether these actually are the key milestones in your life which define who you really are. Live with the list for a little while, mull it over. Once you have refined it and you are happy with it, this is your story.

Review your list – maybe in a year or five years – but currently it is what you are happy to share with people about yourself, right now. It is about giving away an essence of who you are and how you came to be. Remember what I said, it is beautiful to give away an essence of yourself. People trust you and feel privileged and honoured that you have given something of yourself. They get you and they also share more of themselves.

Continues...

Exercise Six continued...

Once you have lived with your story for a while, distil it into a one-sentence strap line of no more than twelve words. Then when people ask you about yourself, that's what you start with: one sentence that gives them an essence of you, your character and who you are. This essence is the beginning of creating connections. You are putting the essence of your story into your business so that people can connect with you.

My Word

My Word – the word that best encapsulates me – is "happiness". I want to continue to be happy and I want other people to be happy. This is my self-actualisation. If I achieve ultimate happiness and get others to that point as well, then I feel that I have achieved everything.

I believe happiness is the ultimate achievement, from which everything else stems. So that is my Word. For my confidence and styling client, her Word is "inspiration". She is a very inspirational person and she wants to inspire other people.

So why is having your Word important? There are times in your life when you are feeling down, you have had a knock, something hasn't worked out and the negative messages are all whirling round in your head; you have lost your foundations. It happens to all of us, it is quite natural.

Sometimes you just need something to reconnect you back to what's important, what you are about, why you are here. Sometimes it is just great to have a Word to re-ground you.

If I am feeling nervous about something, my Word brings me back into my purpose and myself. Without chanting a meandering affirmation all I have to remember is "happiness". For me, happiness is what it is about, my Word returns me to the moment. When I think of my Word my chest tightens and my temperature rises. I have an emotional connection with my Word and that's why it connects me back to who I am.

Finding your Word can do the same for you.

Exercise Seven: Finding Your Word

This is a process of trialling words. It may come out of you automatically. You get an emotional response to your Word, maybe a rise in temperature or a reaction in your glands and you think, "Gosh, where did that come from?" Highlight that word, put it aside, play with it and see if it is something that you remain connected with. Ask yourself, "Is that my Word?"

Everyone is going to have a different Word. Your word captures what is meaningful to you. It doesn't matter what the word is but it is important to find it because your Word will re-ground you. Whatever emotional state you are in, whatever has happened to you, whatever difficulties you face, your Word pulls you back into yourself.

To get you started, look at the following list of words and try some of them out.

Love	*Happiness*	*Inspiration*	*Goodness*
Faith	*Kindness*	*Intelligent*	*Worldly*
Giving	*Relaxed*	*Prosperity*	

There are many more words – find a word that resonates with you and that lifts you.

Finding our core strength

It is interesting that well-rounded people can find it difficult to pull out their uniqueness, their passion, their skills, their word, or their story because they are too close to be objective. It is the same with their core strength. What I mean by core strength is something that is deep down inside of us all that we draw on but do not know where it comes from.

There are things that you do in your life where you discover yourself, you discover things about your core that you had not tested before or did not know you possessed.

There have probably been periods in your life where things have happened and you have reacted in a way that has surprised even yourself. If you have not marked these events, it is time to go back and recognise the core strength you drew on at those times.

A Marathon Story

A few years ago I ran a marathon. I did all the training and I knew that I could get round the course but when it came to it and I was doing it, it was not so easy. I reached about twenty miles and I was struggling; I could have stopped. It would have been easier to stop as I doubted I could finish but I knew there was absolutely no way I was going to stop, there was no way I was going to give up. What was that? I repeated over and over to myself, "One more step, one more step". I had blisters and I was in a lot of pain but what I recognised when I finished was that I had used my core strength.

I learnt something about myself, about my personality that I did not know before. I tend not to give up on things or even people. I knew I could get round the marathon, I could have walked twenty-six miles but running twenty-six miles meant I had to use my core strength to get me to finish; I had to find some strategies. Before I ran the marathon, I <u>thought</u> I wouldn't give up but I didn't <u>know</u> this until I was in the race.

The hippo story

I worked in Africa for a while and at one time I was on a canoe trip going down the Okavango Delta in Botswana when we hit a hippo low in the water. The Mokoro canoe is made of a dug-out tree trunk – it is very heavy and strong; but when we hit the hippo it broke like an eggshell and the next moment we were in the water.

I did not realise there was a hippo in the water but my friend, who was sitting higher in the middle of the Mokoro, had seen it. She went into the foetal position; kept herself down in the water, thinking she was about to be swallowed by a hippo. Then all of a sudden she jumped out of the water, her arms in the air, in shock.

I was just swimming around, collecting the debris around the water, picking up my camera, my boots and all the things that had fallen out of the Mokoro, like I had all the time in the world because I had not realised there was anything dangerous in the water.

I tried to get my friend's attention but she was not focusing. I went over to her to grab her and pull her out; she was looking past me and when I turned to see what she was looking at, I saw the eyes of the hippo disappear in the water and realised I was in his line of fire.

I threw away all of the debris and moved to grab my friend who was fixed in shock, to pull her out. It was funny because we were swimming around but then I realised we could put our feet down, so I literally just dragged her out.

I was giggling nervously. I did not really think it was funny; or rather, it was a disbelieving type of funny.

My friend remained in shock, she was shivering and she had a few bruises. The hippo must have run past her while she was underwater. We couldn't be helicoptered to safety or otherwise get back to the village because it was now late in the day, so we had to stay out all night. We had few clothes, so it was challenging keeping ourselves warm.

The guide who was with us had panicked for fear of repercussions. I was initially unaware we hit a hippo in the water but when I realised, my instinct was to get out fast and I automatically entered action mode. When I came out of the water that survival instinct stopped, but it was there when I needed it. At that moment I learnt that I knew what to do.

I now know that hippos are the most deadly wild animals in Africa!

An incident like that tests us. When something like that happens, we learn about ourselves, but unless you take note of the event, you do not learn who you are and you do not know your capabilities.

I know now that if there is a demanding situation, I will handle myself well, I know that I will know what to do. I do not know why or how I know what to do, I just do. That gives me confidence in my own ability to come through whatever happens.

What do you know about your core strengths?

Exercise Eight: Find your Core Strength

You need to find what your core strength is and it may not be obvious to you. You need to think about how you reacted in various situations, what is it you did? Take time to think about it, to record it.

Recount one or two incidents or events in your life that changed your experience of yourself. Record your SARF:

Situation*:*

Action *you took:*

Result *of your action:*

Feelings *experienced at the time of the event:*

Summarise what core strength you discovered in yourself:

This is a powerful way to know yourself and it gives you the confidence to go forward. You can make a difference in the world through your core strength.

Dig deep, go back and see what you did, how you reacted in a significant situation and mark it down. It is important to know yourself, to trust yourself, to be confident about yourself.

My mantras

Mantras are a useful thing to draw on in times of challenge, a useful shorthand to get a situation in perspective.

My mantras are:

- "You're not going to die": Of course, we all know we are going to die at some point but probably not from this thing, this person, this event, this trouble, this business, this project, this partner, this customer, this day, this month; so you might as well get on with it.
- "Life is too short": So stop wasting time, as soon as you have done it, it is done. Move on! Do everything you want to do and do it now.
- "Take every risk available to you": Clearly do not put yourself in danger but embrace the new and take that leap of faith to that unknown point.
- "The view is better the higher up you get": So when you are down pick yourself up, dust yourself off and keep moving towards the top.

Celebrating

Having gone through these exercises, looked at why it is so important to bring out your personality (so that others can connect with you and you can connect with them), found your Word and your core strength, identified your passion and your unique skills, it's time to celebrate your new awareness.

You are a wonderful person, original and amazing. Tell people about you and celebrate your life! Enjoy who you are and what you are here to do. Do not compare yourself to anyone else because they are completely different, they are not on your path. You have this life to do what you do, so get out there, celebrate it, talk about it and live it.

Chapter four

Purpose

Words may show a man's wit [but] actions his meaning.

Benjamin Franklin

Your business purpose: what business are you in, what is your business focus and why?

Why is it important to find your business purpose? Purpose gives you clarity, and it is very important to have clarity in your business. After all, if you are not clear about what you do, why you do it and the benefits your customers are going to get from it, how do you expect customers to come to you?

The key to business is your customer. It is not about you giving, but about the customer wanting and receiving. What needs are you serving? If you are not clear about those things your business will not be as successful as it could be. If a potential customer comes to you and asks, "What do you do?" or "How do you do it?" that is an indication you have not done a good enough job in making your message clear and succinct and easily understood – whether that's through an image or a phrase.

I meet so many business people who have rehearsed an elevator pitch to introduce their business and after the pitch I still do not understand what they do. The pitch is all very flowery, packed with marketing terms but that essential information is not clear.

What business are you in?

I am a straight talker with entrepreneurs; I ask, "What is it that you do"? If they are this unclear when they introduce their business to me, they are probably just as unclear on their website and in every way that they communicate their business purpose. I may bring to their attention the fact that their message is cloudy.

If you are not clear, most customers will walk away because they will think your business is not for them. This is such a waste! You have got the customers in your sight-line but you are not clear so they walk away. As a business person you cannot afford for that to happen.

Be clear about what business you are in, what needs you serve, what problems you solve and what your business focus is. Be clear in your message as you communicate it. It is absolutely critical that your customer is clear about what you are going to do for them.

Take note of the words you use

When somebody does ask questions, take note of the words and phrases you use in your answers. You can see in the recipient's body language, in their eyes, when they get your point. So ask yourself, "What was the phrase I used that got that reaction"? Make a note so that next time round you lead with that phrase. You want people to say, "I understand it, I get it; I want to buy one of those." You want them to get your lucid message quickly.

There will be different phrases that will attract different types of customers, so experiment with the key words in a particular environment or for a particular type of customer. It is important to be clear about the right words that engage the right people.

Identifying the business focus

It is important to identify the business focus so that customers get what you are going to do for them. At the end of the day, the reason why we are in business is because we want to grow the business, make profits and reach more customers.

A key strategy is to get clarity in your business so more customers come to you because they get it, they know what you do for them; only then will your business grow.

Most businesses are not original

It is quite unusual to come across a business that is unique, highly unusual, truly "niche" or specialised. For most businesses, customers have choice in the same, similar or substitute products or services. One of the best ways to put your head above the parapet is to be clear about exactly what you do for customers. There will be similar businesses but they are not your business, other businesses will not be *exactly* you.

Other similar businesses probably do not have that clarity of phrasing that will engage your customer. If you have done the work and spent some time on this, your business purpose will cut through all of that noise and clutter from other businesses. You have the key thing that your customer is looking for. It is the words that engage them; the kind of words that they themselves would use, because customers know what they need and want and are willing to buy it. This is what you are trying to achieve, that they see or hear your message because it speaks to them.

Target the pain

Be clear about your business focus, be clear about what business you are in, be clear about what needs you serve and what problems you solve and the way that you solve them. In essence what you are doing is identifying your customer's pain so that you can target your solution directly to their pain; so that you can provide the "headache tablet" that will cure their "headache".

Identify your customer's pain so you can target your solution to the customer's need, so that you provide that headache tablet.

How is your business different?

As we said in the last chapter, your personality sets your business apart. Beyond this, your purpose and your business focus create uniqueness around what you do and why you do it.

Define what problem your customers have and what aspect of that problem you can solve consistently.

How do we find our business focus?

Take the example of physiotherapists or indeed many health practitioners. When I asked the physio I worked with, "What business you are in?" I got an explanation of what a physiotherapist is and does. She said she was in clinical health science, she was professional; she rehabilitated and improved movements. Physios tend to be very evidence-based and might talk about natural remedies and so on. Because they are in the medical field, they are often very proud of the jargon, they see medical terms as their mark of quality, credibility and professionalism.

Jargon can clog and clutter a lot of customers' thought processes as they are trying to get to the core of what the practitioner can do for them. Customers generally are not interested in you; they are interested in what you are going to do for them, what you are going to deliver to solve their problem.

Do customers care from one physiotherapist to another about the jargon and medical terminology? This is all about how the solution is going to be delivered. It is too early to talk about that. Once customers get through your door you can talk about how you are going to deliver the solution; first, you need to get them through your door. Focus on the message that will get a customer to find you and to knock down your door.

In the case of the physiotherapist I worked with, I questioned her about why a new potential customer would come to her. The reason new customers go to a physiotherapist is because they are in physical pain. What they need is immediate relief of that physical pain. The physiotherapist is in the business of immediate physical pain relief, like the headache tablet.

In this case, immediacy is key for a new potential customer. A new customer, when motivated to act, will not wait in pain; they want immediate relief. The physiotherapist is in the business of immediate pain relief.

Exercise Nine: What business are you in?

Review your business with these specific points in mind.

Is it clear to my customer what business I am in?

What customer need do I serve?

What pain do I relieve?

Why would a new customer come to my business?

What do existing customers get for their custom that they cannot get elsewhere?

Is the new and existing distinction clear from my marketing message?

Use the answers to these questions to gain clarity on what business you are in and to review your marketing message. Put that message into a key phrase.

Once you gain clarity about the core of your business from the customer's perspective, a lot of the peripheral stuff you do around gaining new customers simply falls away. Your business becomes less cluttered with unimportant activities and messages, which can often be dropped.

You can now use that key phrase as a benchmark for structuring your business and the activities in your business. This enables you to grade what is "critical", what is "important" and what is "not important" in delivering your product or service.

Whatever you do that is core to delivering immediate pain relief to the customer then becomes a priority activity in this business.

In my physio example, once we got clarity about why customers come, a lot of the communication from the business changed. It was so obvious: a sign saying, "Pain relief here!" It was only a few words but it was an exact match for what was going through the head of that new potential customer. It is going to get their attention; you are saying, "I can solve your specific problem". They won't shop around for someone else; they will pick up the phone to you, they will walk into your business, because you have made it clear that you can solve their immediate problem.

In your business, you need to have a phrase that taps into how to motivate a new customer to see your messages above the other 5000+ messages, and walk through your door. Once you have that phrase it becomes so much clearer to you what you do for your customers, and also easier for the customer to understand what you do for them.

You are telling them you can solve their problem in the way they want it solved. Remember, it is not about you it is about the customer.

To summarise, why would a new potential customer come to your business? What need are you serving? What problem are you solving? Keep drilling down until you get to the key phrase of what business you are in.

Why are you in business?

This is a question I often ask my entrepreneurs and business owners and I often get a long pause before they answer. They have to think about it. They know what activities they are involved in, they know their skills, they might even know the passion behind the skills but I am not talking about why you are in business in terms of your passion and skills. What I am talking about is much bigger. This is the big "Why" question - your own unique Why question.

- Why do you have to do what you do?
- Who or what are you doing it for?

The "Why" is bigger than your passion for something, your abilities or your skills. It needs to set your world on fire, it needs to light you up, because if it doesn't light you up it will not light others; so let's do some work on your "Why"? "Why do you do what you do"?

We're looking for the reason that is so strong within you that when you tap into it, you have no choice but to succeed, you have no choice but to do what you do, to your highest ability. Once you have tapped into that "Why", it drives you forward. Whenever you get unfocused and lost, you need to just tap back into why you are doing it.

Your "Why" is bigger than you, it keeps you on your path. It is your motor and it will be unique to you. It is your reason and once you find it and tap into it, its power makes things so much easier. Again it comes back to having clarity of purpose. Once you turn that motor on it just keeps going.

Exercise Ten: What is my true purpose in Life? Getting to my "Why"

Make sure you have 15-20 minutes when you won't be interrupted in order to complete this exercise. Do a Brain Dump and clear your head of social conditioning, perceptions and judgments. Adopt a light, positive frame of mind. Then ask yourself these questions, writing down any answer that pops into your head. Again do not worry about grammar, spelling and proper sentences:

If you could do anything, what would it be?

Why would you do it?

Why would it matter?

Who or what would you do it for?

Why do you need to do it?

What is different about it?

What is in you, your experience, your values, your knowledge, your skills, your technique, your passion, your opinion, your motivation, etc?

Continues...

Exercise Ten continued...

If you did not do what you do, who would care, what would they miss out on and why?

Why you?

Why are you compelled to do it?

Who are you doing it for?

Once you have answers to these questions, move on and ask:

Why is that important to me?

What is it about that that's important to me?

What will it give me if I do this?

Why should I do this?

Keep drilling down, keep asking these questions, to the point where you have no more answers.

How you know when you've got to your "Why"

The answers at this point should give you a very strong emotional pull. There should almost be an emotional hurt or tightness. If the answer doesn't make you want to cry or feel deep emotions then you have not got your "Why". When you have got to your "Why" you will have a strong emotional connection to it. If you're not there yet, keep going; keep asking the questions till you feel that emotional pull. The emotional feeling might be in your gut, it might be in your heart or your throat; there will be a part of your body that will react.

Once you have got it, walk away and come back the next day and tap into the answer again, so that you feel that emotional pull. If it is there the next day you know you are in the right place.

When you are feeling uncertain, when you are feeling a bit doubtful, your "Why" is there for you to tap into again, to turn on the engine again so you are firing and ready to go. Everything you do gets easier. You are removing uncertainty; you absolutely know with certainty that you are going to achieve success. There's no choice once you have your "Why". Once you have recognised what it is, you are compelled to do it, you have no choice: it is set. Do not judge, do not worry about HOW, just trust in yourself and know it is right.

Purpose is about clarity and focus and with it, everything is easy.

If you're not finding your "Why" easily...

Everyone has a "Why" but sometimes it is difficult to tap into that emotional pull. Ask someone close to you: they may see you better than you see yourself and often new stimulus gives a new perspective. With this new stimulus, start your "Why" questions again.

Whilst it is good to get the views of someone close, be cautious of other people's perceptions of you. People who love us want to keep us safe and secure. So frame your enquiries well and do not let others limit your thinking and define your dream. Do not ask their permission to dream big but get their insight into your unique skills and abilities, things that may not be obvious to you.

For many parents, their "Why" is their child. For me, it is my sister. She is the closest person to me; she is my "Why". Whenever I feel down and I have not got enough energy to do it for myself, I can do it for her. It took me a while to find my "Why" – it was not initially obvious to me. I had to re-visit this a few times, I spoke to a few people about this subject, about finding their "Why" and in talking about it I felt some surprising emotional pulls which I investigated later to come up with my own "Why".

Gently persist without judgment

Speaking to other people about my "Why" was interesting because I could see clearly whether or not they had found their "Why". Many were still in their head and not in their heart. You cannot think your "Why"; you have to feel it.

This is a result of social conditioning; things that our parents have told us, things that we think that we should be and should do. It is like an onion: sometimes it takes a while to get rid of the layers of who you thought you should be, of what you thought you should be doing or of trying to live up to your parents' or your partner's expectations. Peeling away these layers does take a little bit of work and there may be tears.

For some people it comes easier than others but it is important to do that work and tap into it, get rid of the perception that people have of us and we have of ourselves.

If this is a new idea to you, be easy on yourself and do not expect to reach your "Why" at your first attempt. Remember, you may have to peel back a few layers of perception. If you have not found that pull of emotion, trust that it will eventually come. Do not give up on it, your "Why" is of the upmost importance.

Knowing your "Why" is the difference between paddling in your boat using physical effort to move forward, or switching on your engine to move effortlessly. With clarity and focus your path becomes clear.

Growing business vs. maintaining business

In finding your purpose in this chapter, we have been talking about new potential customers. In the last P, Process, we look at how your processes can either lose customers or maintain and grow existing customers. There are different strategies that you would use with existing customers.

Business growth is about getting people to your door, and also getting customers who are already through your door to come on a regular basis, to buy more, more often. Clarity in finding your business focus, what business you are in, is critical for both activities.

Growing your business with your existing customer base includes up-selling: having premium products or another level that your customers can upgrade to and also cross-selling a wider range of products, either in-house or through joint venture and partnership arrangements. It is important to maintain your relationships with your existing customers, keeping them happy, keeping a dialogue at whatever level that individual customer might want. Too often businesses focus on new and overlook existing customer relationships; you must keep them engaged, look after them, make them feel valued.

I often see in business that the head of the business may prefer to focus on bringing in new customers, to be at the forefront of the business, and they might have staff, mechanisms and systems in place to maintain customers.

Clarity in what business you are in works on both levels in that it will bring in new customers because they are clear about what you will do to solve their problem, and it also helps to create loyalty with existing customers because they know they are in the right place.

Becoming the expert

Once you are clear about your business focus, you become the expert; even other people in your field look up to you, and ask why are you are doing so well, or why you are so knowledgeable, so self-assured? Clarity and confidence oozes out of you.

Once you have clarity it is easier for you to become the expert, the go-to person for your sector. All the relevant information finds you, and it is easier for others to give you referrals and recommendations. These come not only from your customers, but also from suppliers or other people you deal with. They listen and understand the clear message of what business you are in and they can make connections. Once you also have clarity of purpose around what you do, what you do not do, what needs you serve, it is easier for you to get support in your business.

It also makes space in your mind; you have gotten rid of the clutter, the peripheral stuff that has no importance in your business. Your competitors are looking at you because you have that clarity. They do not know what drives you but they know there is a difference. It also infects your customers, both potential and existing. It is absolutely powerful; it is brilliant.

This has certainly worked in my own personal experience; the planets align to bring me what I need when I need it. When I speak to business owners, also, and help them to identify what business they are really in, that focus and clarity gives them permission and certainty.

A gift shop or a craft shop?

An example of the power of gaining this clarity was with a business owner who had a craft shop on a high street. The shop was filled with the things the owner thought would be of interest to their customers, but actually, the items were of interest to the owner, who was passionate about cake-making and craft-making. The business sold gifts, cards and crafts but struggled to break-even; the average sale value was low.

The problem was that the business owner did not know what business she was in: a gift business or a craft business.

After much questioning and listening, we identified that the core of this business is "spending time". Why buy a cake when you can spend time lovingly making a cake? Why buy a card when you can make a personal gift? Why buy a gift when you can spend time making something that creates much more value? Her products were aimed at people who thought like this. What a wonderful gift she gave to her customers, to help them to spend quality time lovingly making personal gifts that someone else would value for longer than a second.

So now, her shop is no longer just a High Street shop competing with others, it is a beacon of love, it is a suspension of time, it is something you share. Do you think this realisation would energise the owner's passion to focus and grow her business?

The business message

As individuals we are multi-talented, well-rounded people. Sometimes business people make the mistake that when they introduce themselves, they introduce three types of business. All that tells me is that they are a master of none, that they do not want to turn away any business so they will say "Yes" to everything. They do not have clarity and focus.

Without clarity it is difficult for me to help them, or to recommend their business to my contacts. They may be able to do everything, but can they do it all to an optimal level?

Focus on the core of your business.

In my case, my core message is, "I am in the business of business growth, the reason entrepreneurs and business owners come to me is that they want to take their business to the next level and do not know how."

The "how" will be different for each business, because each owner, business and customer segment is unique, and so their problems and solutions are unique.

The business owner's problem may be that they are not making enough money or cash flow is limited in the business, it may be they do not have enough customers or enough sales volume. There may be a whole host of different reasons, but the core to this is they all want to grow their business. So I help grow businesses.

The way I deliver business growth will depend on the needs of the business, the problem, the location, the sector, the individual. It is never a one-size-fits-all solution, but it is all about business growth.

In speaking to the business owner I tap into the specific problem that concerns them – I would give a case study of a past client in a similar industry, or in a similar situation.

When I conduct speaking engagements, however, I say that, "I help businesses grow by motivating thinking into action", because I am giving them an insight, experience or training which will help them think differently. I do not say, "I am in the business of business growth" because at that point I am not physically in front of the business.

I do not want the entrepreneurs who are attending to think, "Oh, that was wonderful, inspirational", and walk away and continue to do what they have always done and get the same results. They are sitting there because they have got a problem that needs solving or they want to learn something new.

I aim to give the audience an insight that changes their thinking or a strategy that they can take away that day and apply to their business. There will be a whole host of different types of businesses attending, so I have to give them a nugget that is generic enough for them all to use.

In this case, my priority is to motivate their thinking about growing their business to a point that makes it easy, so they can apply the insight and ideas right away in their business. In that context, I aim to help them make a difference on their path to growing their business by changing thinking, not behaviours.

Align your message to your audience

You would not use the same phrase to attract new customers as you would to communicate with existing customers. However the core, the over-riding message is the same – in my case, business growth. I am in the business of business growth. How I deliver the messages will change with the audience – new or existing customers – and with the delivery method – speaking presentations or one-to-one or small group consultancy/mentoring.

Align your message to your distribution channel

You may have different distribution channels, for example you may sell some of your products online, some face-to-face, some may be physical and some may be digital products. You use different language, different phrases, in each of these situations; the core product is the same but the audience may be different and so the message is sensitive to the audience and channel.

Align your message

"*Cognitive empathy*" is a way of tuning in to another person. It gives us an understanding of their view but also gives us indicators of how best to communicate with them on their wavelength. It is not important what you think. It is, however, important what your customer thinks and says. Cognitive empathy allows you to choose what words to use and what words to avoid in communicating your message.

Managers with excellent cognitive empathy, for instance, get better than expected performance from their direct reports. And executives who have this mental asset do well when assigned to a culture different than their own – they are able to pick up the norms and ground rules of another culture more quickly.[13]

There are clear benefits in the use of cognitive empathy to align your message, engage your audience and make things easy for your customer by talking your customer's language so they get what they want.

Do not make the customer work out what you do

If your customer has to work out what you do, you have already lost them. Why would you expect your customer to do the work? That is your job. It is your responsibility to deliver your message to them clearly.

It is great when you get feedback on this, when a customer says, "Hang on a moment, I do not understand".

That is fantastic feedback, because it gives you the opportunity to test and refine your message and see where you missed the mark.

Even when you get a complaint, ask the customer for more information so you can make sure you understand what went wrong and correct it, and what you did that was great so you can do that more for more customers. You may have put something out in the market and the customer did not understand that particular product, purchased it and then found it was the wrong product.

The fault is not the customer's; it is yours. When you get that feedback, embrace it, and clarify your message with their feedback. The customer is coming to your door, willing to exchange money for your products and services. Appreciate that they have done a lot of work to get this far.

Your job is to make it absolutely clear to them what you do and why you are doing it and what they should expect to receive. You want them to think, "I get it, I want it, I am going to buy it", not, "What is it? How does it work? Why should I buy this? What benefits am I going to get?"

It is okay to make a mistake, but learn fast, embrace the feedback, even solicit it. Do not waste your energies out there in the market with an unclear message. Make sure when you get out there that you are clear, that you make it easy for your customers to say, "I want one of those".

If you have three or four things you do, how do you choose which one is your core message?

This comes back to your "Why". Once you have your big "Why", probably only one or two out of the four things really fulfil that big "Why". That will help you narrow down the options and focus your energies.

When assessing what business you want to be in, there are quantitative and qualitative measures that you can look at. A good starting point is the customer, the audience – is there any money in this market? At the end of the day we all need to live; and not only survive – the more money you make, the more you can contribute.

Is there a big enough need in your market? Is your message powerful enough? Are there enough people who want what you are selling? If not, it doesn't mean you shouldn't do what you are doing, but you may need to structure your business differently.

For example, if you are a local business, in a local community, and you have an idea for a business but there are not enough people in the local community to make money out of it, you may be able to structure it to be an online business. There may be enough people in the wider world community who want that particular product or service for your business to be a success. When you're thinking about your business structure, your "Why" will help you to narrow down your focus.

If you are equally as passionate about all your business interests, then look at which of the market segments are going to allow you to grow your business quickest.

Once you have narrowed down to one activity, you need to focus. Put the others aside and focus on that one. Sometimes that can be quite difficult, emotionally. Business owners are often passionate about a whole host of things – which is why I do not use passion to narrow down what business you should be in.

This is where you can use the big "Why". Once you have narrowed it down and you have made the decision to stick with this one business going forward, this allows you to make your difference a lot quicker. You have total focus and commitment to that business, you will be attracting more customers, more connections simply because you are completely clear about what business you are in.

Once you have made a success of that – and you *are* going to make a success of it – you can branch out and follow the other passions if you still feel passionate about them. You can structure your business so that you have a manager, and then you can leverage the success of the first business to launch the second business, which will grow quicker from the experience of the first.

Why is that the case? Because you have already done all the hard work in the first business, you have developed your market, you have developed your reputation, you have developed your expertise, you have a following of customers who know you and trust you.

Even if it is a completely different product or market, they trust you so you can say, "Hey, look, I recommend you try this because I have used it and I believe in it". You are more likely to get people to buy it because they believe in you, they have some experience and some history with you.

Jo Malone

A great example of this is Jo Malone who grew her business from a kitchen table over twenty years and sold Jo Malone, a luxury fragrance business, to Estee Lauder in 1999. Now after battling cancer she opened Jo Loves in 2011. "This time round", however, "she's not selling a lifestyle She's selling a persona and a personality: her own. A warm, funny, compassionate personality that has [us] laughing and crying in sympathy, all within the space of an hour".[14] Jo is getting a great deal of attention on the back of her story, her reputation, one that she built while growing her first business. Based on her wealth of experience she is easily able to tune-in to who is her customer and what they want. She is focused and clear about how Jo Love will develop, benefiting from lessons honed in previous business experience.

You will not start at the beginning with the second business, you already have the reputation; both businesses will develop quicker when you focus on them one at a time.

Cognitive empathy allows us to get on the same wave-length or tune in, giving us a sense of how another person's thinking works. It is one of three kinds of empathy, each with a premium in the workplace and in relationships anywhere in our lives.

This way of tuning in to another person does more than give us an understanding of their view – it tells us how best to communicate with that person: what matters most to them, their models of the world, and even what words to use – or avoid – when talking with them.

Tuning in pays off in many ways.

Creating a brand story

Your brand story leverages the work you did in the Personality chapter, where we talked about putting your unique characteristics into your business. You can use some elements of this when creating your brand story.

The importance of having a brand story is that customers like transparency: they like to know who they are dealing with, who is behind the business, and what you stand for. You may not necessarily be the face of the company but they want to know who is leading it.

Having a brand story is brilliant for filling the gaps and building trust. Some of it may be not be directly relevant to your business, but it all works to create credibility; it portrays a rounded, trusted character. Think of Jo Malone's story: being told that she had only months to live will resonate with many others. It has nothing to do with fragrance but everything to do with her personality, her determination in life is no different than her determination in business.

If you are a parent, that may not have relevance to your business, but it gives a complete picture of you. It is your choice what you want to put out there. Which of your life experiences will work best for you? You have some influence over what is out in the public domain, so take control by putting what you want out.

The most important question to answer, once again, is your "Why". Why are you so passionate about what you do? What makes you jump out of bed in the morning to do it? Also include some background information. You might tell the story of what started you on this particular path. It may be an incident in your life – even a negative incident – which caused you to stop and re-assess where you were heading, and made you think, "I want something else out of life, I want to do this, I want to share this with people, I need to do this" or "this is my unique skill". This may be the start of your brand story.

Make sure you are comfortable with what you are going to say, but also make sure you make it engaging and beneficial to the customer. It is about getting customers to see why you are out there doing what you do in such a way that they want to engage with you.

Why tell your story?

Customer testimonials only tell part of the story. They highlight what you have already put out there, give evidence that you can do what you say; your story tells them something more. It relates to why you do what you do and why you are the person to solve your customer's problem; what values you share and how your shared experience meets their need.

I met a wonderful yoga teacher who does very energising yoga. Her story is that she had multiple sclerosis, so now she trains other yoga teachers to help people with multiple sclerosis. Her story comes from a point of having lived and breathed the illness and having conquered it: "I have had this disease, this yoga practice has worked for me and I want to share it with the world so that people do not have to go through the pain, the isolation, the feeling that nothing can be done. You do not have to live with this debilitating illness for the rest of your life."

CREATING GROWTH IN A RAPIDLY CHANGING WORLD

Her story is that you do not have to be satisfied with where you are at this moment, there are things you can do to change your position in life. Her personal experience is that it works and she can teach you how to do it.

So that's her story. What is your story? Her story taps into the needs of a particular group of customers. How can you tap into the needs of your customers?

Telling your brand story helps to engage your customer so they see the benefits of working with you. You are coming from a place of passion or experience or knowledge; or perhaps you are engaging because you are humorous or have an unusual perspective.

You want to create a story of a transparency in business that has character and personality behind it.

Exercise Eleven: Create your Brand Story

Your brand story is not the same as your big "Why". Although it relates to you, it is the story which relates to your business activity.

Answer:

Why are you passionate about what you do?

What is it about this that makes you jump out of bed in the morning to do it?

Why are you compelled to share your unique skill?

What will your customers get from it that they cannot get anywhere else?

Once you have the answers to these questions, write them into a statement from the customer's point of view so it engages your customer.

For example: Honest Burgers brand story:

> A **simple** and honest **London** burger restaurant inspired by **Great British produce**. The owners speak of working hard to give their customers what they want and their differentiating factor being their **transparency**, their **honesty** and their **independence** over the chains. [15]

Where do I use my brand story?

Once you have created your brand story, you can record it onto video for your web homepage; you may go out into the market and tell your story, become an evangelist or expert in your field. This works because it is attracting and engaging – you will be amazed at how many people are interested in your story, which is really the reason why your customer would want to buy from you.

You may think you're not that interesting but people are interested in people, they want to know about you: the what and why. Help your customer to understand by getting your message out there. Then you may end your brand story with evidence from existing customers who testify to the benefits or results of what you do.

How finding your business purpose feeds into business growth

Finding your business purpose becomes the fuel behind your business growth. We have previously talked about finding your "Why". That is your engine to turn on full power with purpose and committed vision. You are passionate and firing on all cylinders – that's good, but you might still be a bit directionless, without a rudder. You are energised but if you do not know the route, or which way is north or south, you are spending energy going nowhere fast.

It is important to have your "Why" as the engine behind you; it is also important to have the clarity of knowing why – that's your compass. Your rudder, however, gives you the route and real clarity of what business you are in, for your suppliers, your stakeholders and your customers. This is what goes into the brand story.

The point is, you want your customer to say: "I get it, I want it, I am going to buy it, this is for me".

Coming back to the question of, "What business I am in, what need do I serve, what problem do I solve?" The answers are the guiding beacon that gives you a clear direction of where you are going.

Clear out the clutter so you have a direct path to business growth and your customer has a direct path to you.

Chapter five

Pleasure

The aim of marketing is to know and understand the customer so well the product or service fits him and sells itself.

Peter Drucker

"What is your pleasure sir?"

I love the subject of pleasure! It is about mindset. It is about getting under the skin of your customer (cognitive empathy, as mentioned in the previous chapter) and it is about the service that you are here to provide through knowing your customer's wants. You are here to serve your customers.

Even if you are selling a product you are in the service industry. Without your customers you do not have a business; so business is about asking, "How do I serve my customer?" "How can I solve their problem?" "What can I do for you, Madam?" "What is your pleasure, Sir?"

Once you start to work through this and get under the skin of your customer, it is absolutely magical. As before, what you want is for your customer to say, "I want one of those, that fits me, I get it". This chapter is about getting a lot closer to your customer, so your customer wants what you have.

You are not pushing your product onto your customer, your customer wants your product because it fits their needs, they get it and it suits them. You are speaking to their pleasure: their aspirations, their desire. When you use these types of words you automatically feel uplifted and engaged.

The first step is establishing customers' pleasures, their aspirations, their desires. When you ascertain your customers' desires, you also find out their needs. Your job then is to satisfy their wants and their needs. Sigmund Freud's psychoanalytic theory of personality states that, "The id is the personality component made up of unconscious psychic energy that works to satisfy basic urges, needs, and desires. The id operates based on the pleasure principle, which demands immediate gratification of needs".[16]

How does Freud's "pleasure principle" apply to business?

The "pleasure principle" is about how we seek out pleasure and we avoid pain. Accordingly, it is a strong basic urge which drives our id or personality so the motivation for wants and desire, pleasure, and aspirations is greater than our motivation for pain, fear and unfulfilling physiological drivers. In communication with our customer it is important we understand and speak to our customer's desires, wants and pleasure to tune-in to their strong motivating urges. We fulfil our customer's needs when we motivate them with their wants and desire.

For example, the safest car in the world, Volvo's new V40, has recorded the highest ever score in the Euro NCAP crash safety test. Although this is a great accolade, the safety record does not inspire my desires. Volvo for many years has won the safety badge of honour, feeding into the fear (pain) of parents wanting to protect their children while travelling to and from school. These parents are willing to pay a premium to fill the pain need.

The problem for Volvo is that the safety accolade has labelled the company boring, boxy and bland. In leading the safety race the company forgot that even parents have desires, they have dreams and that is not being boring, old and retired! Realising that Volvo was losing key customers, now Volvo is working hard to be edgy, with the introduction of a series of stunts in this summer's advertisements, in an effort to win over younger, sporty and fun people.

Businesses must be in touch with the desires of their customer segments, to motivate them to buy from your business, to enable your customers to achieve their desires and meet their needs.

In Volvo's case, one part of the message speaks to the pain, the need to "keep my children safe" – I know I need

CREATING GROWTH IN A RAPIDLY CHANGING WORLD

to do it but I want more, I deserve more: "I want to strut down the road flaunting what I've got". This speaks to my aspirations, my desires and my pleasure.

Safety has now become a "hygiene factor", something which could lose the sale if it is not there, but not something that wins the sale. Desires are motivating factors, the things we want but do not necessarily need. Without motivating factors we will not buy. These are the emotional triggers that business owners, marketers and sellers must meet for customers to buy.

It is important to speak to your customer in their words, words that will motivate and inspire them. You speak to their aspirations, their desires, to their pleasure.

Customers are much more savvy than they used to be to the traditional fear-based techniques. Pain has less energy over time so customers are less likely to sustain motivation to take action.

When it comes to comparing pain to pleasure, it takes a lot more energy for people to work up the motivation to carry out actions they know will be painful or to stick to their goals; speaking to their pleasures and desires is motivating, both with existing and potential customers.

BUSINESS EVOLUTION

By addressing pleasures, you get past the barriers we all create in our minds about things we know we "should" do, but that we do not want to do. Saying "I should" probably identifies a need, but not a motivating want. Such a lament is the sound of someone beating themselves up. "Should" is the sound of the lash of the whip. It is a feeling of lack, of "trying" to do something; but there is no energy there because there is no motivation, and so failure is likely.

"Should" means, "I am obligated to do it but I am not motivated to do it so I am setting myself up to fail". If someone says, "I want to do this" or, "This is my aspiration", it is energising. The energy is already there, in their words, in their visions of what they want and desire. They have a picture of where they want to be and in their minds they are already there, they are already connected with that energy and the desire to get there. Consequently, it doesn't take much extra energy to carry out the action.

We want to speak our customers pleasure – how do we find out what that is?

Finding your customers' pleasure is easy: the best way to understand and get close to your customers' desire is to ask them! It is as simple as that. But in order to ask them, you need to be very clear about who your customers are and where you can find them.

It takes a little bit of work to determine who your ideal customer is. Ask yourself, what or who energises you? What groups do you enjoy working with? If it is a group of people that you enjoy working with, it makes the work that much easier. Who wants and needs your service or product, whether they know it or not? Sit down and take some time to look at who is your ideal customer, and build a customer profile.

Exercise Twelve: Ideal customer profile

Your existing client bank or customers can be a good place to start. Identify who you enjoy working with and why, what their characteristics are and whether there are more customers like these.

Give that ideal customer a name, then write down the customer's characteristics: they may be single, they may be married, they may be within a certain age group, they may be a certain gender, income level, educational level, ethnicity ...

What is their lifestyle? How long have they been with you as a customer? If it is a long tenure, what is the value of their investment? Are they regular purchasers or are their purchases big but less frequent?

What level of engagement do you have with your ideal customer? Is it little and often, involved and protracted, face-to-face, via email or via social media? Analyse your customer relationships and characteristics looking for similarities and differences and then segment your customers into four groups, naming and describing each segment.

Once you have described the four segments, you are beginning to build up a picture of who your customers are. Prioritise your segments in terms of which are the most valuable and concentrate on your top two.

Then, using a demographic and geo-demographic (location) classification profiler, look for more customers with matching characteristics to those in your top two segments.

How many of your existing customers are ideal? This process is about recognising the key characteristics within the top two segments of your existing client bank that can carry across to a new range of customers who fit your ideal profile and therefore are customers you will enjoy working with.

It may be that you have a whole variety of customers. It may be that most of your high net worth or high value customers, the ones who bring you most of your business, tend to be in a certain location, a certain industry sector, or have a certain educational level, a certain characteristic, a certain lifestyle or certain interests. Whatever it may be, this is not only going to be your ideal customer, but forms the profile of your target customers as well.

Once you have this information, it much easier for you to get closer to your ideal customer because you know who they are and how to find them. You know what age they are, how much they earn, their location and environment and, if they are existing customers, you know how often they buy from you. This means you can begin to target more people like them.

If your customers are businesses, your research would look at size and value of company, number of employees, business structure, industry sector and buying pattern to find the characteristics of your ideal business customer.

At the moment, though, the key thing to do is to get closer to them; interview them in order to find out more about their desires. Perhaps you could take a few of your customers individually out for lunch. On a larger scale, you can email a questionnaire to customers asking some carefully tailored questions to enable you to find out more about them. Surveys are renowned for their poor response rates. However, if you give customers something as a thank you in anticipation of their completing the questionnaire and you get across the purpose of the exercise (your desire to provide a service more aligned to their wants and needs), customers will be more inclined to complete the survey. This research will enable you to "fish where the fish are" - in the right pond with the right bait (more about this later).

Do not assume

Do not assume that your customer is happy with your product and service just because they buy from you. Do not assume you know all about them. It is amazing how many entrepreneurs think that because customers are doing business with them, this means they know their customers and know why their customers shop with them.

It could be that your customers are looking for alternative suppliers, or are shopping with you for a completely different reason than you think. Once you find out that reason you will almost certainly be able to capitalise on this information and win more business or more similar customers. Do not assume. If you want to get close to your customers, ask them questions.

Where to spend your money to bring your customers in

This information about customers' desires helps you to ascertain where you should be spending more of your money in order to bring in more ideal customers.

You need to clarify what your customers' desires are and what language you could use in order to inspire, not only them, but more people like them. Record the words *they* use in the interviews and questionnaires, not yours. Do not assume your understanding is the same as their meaning.

Have the mind of an enquiring child, non-judgemental. Keep asking, "Why is that? Why does that work for you?" and do not judge it, just be open and receive the information that your customer gives you, as a gift.

If you start judging it, you will not drill down far enough to get to the gold, the real nugget of information that could create a real opportunity in your business. Receive the information as they choose to give it, in the words that they choose to give it, and then at a later stage, re-examine it, to see what you can learn from it and where the opportunities lie.

Building up an ideal customer profile and learning from asking questions of your ideal customers can help you grow your business, get more of the customers you want, keep your existing customers happy and improve the way you communicate with them all. Interviews or seeking feedback are a key part of seeking to give your customer pleasure.

Fish where the fish are

This is one of my favourite phrases. You have to know what fish you are looking for; this is why putting together a customer profile is absolutely critical, otherwise you are going to throw out the wrong bait and catch the wrong fish.

Know what you are looking for and do the work to find out who your best customers are: who do you love doing business with? What type of fish are they?

Then you can find out where your fish hang out, whether they are cold-water fish, deep-sea fish or shallow-water fish – or are they somewhere in a fish bowl?

If your ideal customers are parents within a particular location, it might be best to fish on Mumsnet[17] or other sites that attract your profile of customers; it might be Twitter or Facebook; or participating in Parent Teacher Associations or children's play groups. There are lots of forums for your profile of customers which may be good places to share your message. If your ideal customers are technology businesses, perhaps Linkedin,[18] Campus Party,[19] women in technology, TechUK or other technology associations are where you need to cast your line. Where to fish is something you can ask your existing ideal customers in a questionnaire, or when you are face to face. Where do they hang out? This can give ideas as to where you can meet more people like them, so you can fish in the right pond.

Using the right bait

If you know your fish then you know which body of water to find them in. Next you need to know the bait you need to reel them in. Once you know your ideal customers and where they hang out, all you need to do is cast the right line to bring them to your business. This is about communicating well, speaking to their desires and their pleasures; using their language, not yours.

It is important to have the right bait on your line for your fish, that is, the right communication message bespoke to the fish you want to attract.

Now you know where your customers are, how do you reach them? It is good to set up systems in your business so you are constantly engaging with your customer in an intelligent way. This is not just one-way but two-way communication.

One example of communicating with your customers is through competitions. Competitions are not just to give something away; they are also to get something back. You will have already worked out what you want to receive in return – it may be an exchange of information for a chance to win a prize. People have to answer questions to enter and the answers to those questions can give you a lot of valuable information, information you can use to develop your business or perhaps to develop a new product or service.

Competitions are not just a great way to get publicity and create awareness – you can do that anyway with a press release; competitions are a great way to get information and to help you to understand and get closer to your customer.

Use your touch points to gather information

Every touch point with the customer, whether online or face-to-face, is an opportunity for you to gather a bit more information, to get a bit closer to them; this information is going to help you to do a better job in serving them.

Remember, the focus is, "What's your pleasure sir? I am here to serve you." It is about doing what you do better for your customer. Ask your customers open questions. These are excellent for getting more information about their desires and aspirations.

It might be that the customer doesn't realise this questioning has anything to do with the exchange of business. The question might be, "Who is your role model and why?" This will give you lots of aspirational information about your particular customer segment and who they identify with.

Closed questions have their place too and can help you find out information about customers specific needs. For instance, with a weight-loss business, asking, "What is your ideal weight?" But you may not get an answer. Customers may see this as personal and private information (particularly if your questionnaire is not anonymous) and not respond. A more useful question might be: "How much over your ideal weight are you?" This is more likely to garner a response and give you information you can use in further communication with your customers. If they would like to be three inches smaller around the waist, or five kilograms lighter, then you start using that figure in your communication. You can then tell customers this is specifically what you can help them with. You do it in an inspiring way but you use the figures already in the minds of your customers.

Giving your customers information and education

Blogging is a great way to reach out to your customers. When you ask them questions and they tell you what they are interested in, you can write your blogs around this. You can educate them in areas where they want information and education, and receiving valued information will help create a connection to you and your business. If you are a source of useful information, you become the expert, and customers engage with you further because you are giving them what they want and need.

Use information gathered through enquiries as well as competitions and feedback. Every touch point, every point where a customer may contact you, buy from you, leave feedback, is an opportunity to ask open and closed questions, questions that give you more information so you can better serve your customer.

This is important throughout your business. Consistently gather information in order to fine-tune what and how you deliver your product, to solve your customers' problems.

You might want to gather information on their perspective, how they value you against your competition. You may pick up information about your customers' frustrations in a related area and if there is enough demand, this might be an opportunity for new product development.

You may have a new product that you want to launch. Before you launch it, you might have a competition to name the product. You could ask your customers to critique the new product while in its development stage and so your customers help to improve the prototype and possibly become the buyers of this new product. This can save a lot of time, energy and money, developing a product through the engagement and with the help of a specific customer segment. The customer feels they are more of a part of your company and it gives you an opportunity to communicate with them again, to thank them for their information. You may give them a reward for that very valuable information. Remember, free information – even a complaint – is a valuable gift.

This is all done within your ideal customer segment, you are learning more and more about your customers all the time. There are great marketing strategies to get you closer to your customer so you can do what you do even better and grow your business further. It is important to be knowledgeable and crystal clear about what you do for your customer that no one else can do in the way you do it; and also to understand your customers' wants and needs because ultimately this is the key to the success of your business.

Where does brand come into this conversation?

For the customers you already have, there may be aspects within your brand that they engage with, but you might not know what those aspects are. What are the characteristics within your brand that engage them? What is it about the offering that they like?

It is important to identify these things, because there may be some things that are just not hitting the mark with the customer. The only way of finding this out is, again, to ask them. You can use some of the strategies we have talked about to fine-tune your brand and how it is perceived, perhaps changing some of those characteristics or bringing other aspects that you thought were less important to the fore. You are engaging more, your message is clearer to your customer. Use these information-gathering strategies to refine and develop your brand.

How do we communicate with the customer?

We know where the customers are and we know what their needs are; we have removed the barriers that we as entrepreneurs sometimes put up, so that now we are engaging our customers better. We have started to use our customers' own words, so that we speak to them in their own voice.

Now in the communication we need to work out what questions our customers are asking, so we can provide simple and easy solutions for them. We need to understand what frustrations we are easing and how our customers feel.

When you question your customers, you get to speak to their wants, their desires, their pleasures and the things that appeal to them. How you communicate with them is about the words you use. In our earlier examples, "I can help you keep up with your kids" or "I can make you look great in jeans", the words used were words that came from your customer aspirations, the actual words they use. It depends on what industry sector you are in, your particular ideal customer and what their aspirations are.

This is something to play with and continue evolving. When you are in front of a customer and they use a word, phrase or certain terminology, start using it straightaway yourself. Do not feel that once you have landed on terminology that is good, and that works, that you will use it forever. Your message should keep evolving all the time, through every interaction and every conversation with each customer segment.

The language we use changes over time, so to remain relevant with the various customer segments, your message will change over time. You might have one customer segment that is your ideal customer and another customer segment you come across that also has a need or desire for your product. The motivating desires may be quite different, so going back to the weight-loss example, one customer segment may be single with a style aspiration – to look great in jeans – and the other customer segment may be parents, wanting to keep up with their kids – more a fitness aspiration than a diet one.

You might develop different motivating messages for various customer segments. One size of jean will not fit all your customers and one message will not suit them all. It is important to segment your market and deliver the right message for each segment of customers. Do a customer profile for all the different customer segments in your business that you value and want to grow. On your website, for instance, think about having a different page that will motivate each group – have a bounteous supply of jeans for every occasion ensuring the segment has a direct link to their message!

To summarise:
- Use your customers' words, not your own.
- Have an open, enquiring mind and do not assume that you already know the answers.
- Speak to your customers' pleasure; speak to their aspirations and their desire.
- Do not speak only to their pain or need because you are not going to sustain the motivation of the customer.
- Tap into the wants and desires of each unique customer segment.

Speak to the customer

As business owners we are involved and passionate about our businesses and we want to do well for our customers. However, we do not always have the customer's perspective in mind. We naturally have our own business perspective in mind and it is difficult to take ourselves out of this mindset. But it is critical to do this if you want to grow your business and remain relevant to your customer. You must think like your customers. This is a key element missing in many businesses today.

One way of viewing your business from your customers' perspective is to take the customer journey yourself, to get an insight to your customers' experience of your business.

Let me give you an example of not having predictive perspective. When I am working on written material, I know what I want to say but as I type my fingers do not move fast enough to capture all the thoughts that are going through my mind. So I make mistakes. But when I read and re-read the document, my brain fills in the words that I have missed in the text, I fail to spot some of the silly errors that my spell checker does highlighted. It is not until a day or so later, when I have taken a break from the text, that I spot the previously unnoticed but now obvious mistakes. It is very infuriating that my brain fills in the gaps, rather like "predictive text".

We do use predictive perspective in business all the time. We fill in the gaps and are blind to the problems our customers face in doing business with us. We assume and know how we want to perform and so we do not see the mistakes. We do not see the gaps because we know the process, so our mind and ego fills the gap.

This is why it is so difficult to turn your business around and look at it from the customer point-of-view, you are constantly filling in the obvious gaps that customers see and experience; you actually do not see them at all.

Look at another, similar business

One way of taking yourself out of the predictive perspective of your business is to go to another similar business and take the customer journey there. When you look at another business with a critical eye, you will not be filling in the gaps. It is a good way of looking for opportunities to improve your own business, as it highlights similar gaps in your own business and opens your mind to new opportunities.

But you have to be open and honest about all of this process. This is not about you, it is about growing your business by finding and filling the gaps. Once you see the gaps, ask your customers: "Have you experienced this?" They probably won't come up to you and say, "This is terrible", but if you ask if they have experienced the problem, they are more likely to tell you honestly "yes" or "no". Then you can ask how they would suggest you improve and with this information you can start to fill the gap and resolve the blind spot.

In visiting similar businesses (hopefully one where they do not know you) record your experience from the first touch point to the last. Critique that business: could the process have been easier, could it be made better and if so, how? Then take the knowledge you have gained into your own business and look at the different touch points and improve them. Look at any gaps and think how you could fill those blind-spots to aid your customer, to make the process simpler, more in flow, more succinct, easier.

Look at the message the similar business gives their customers and see where there may be ambiguity and room for more clarity, then make that improvement in your own business. Did this business meet their claimed service standard? Have the courage to look at your business honestly.

You may be feeling uncomfortable about this. The purpose behind it goes back to service: "How can I serve you?" This is not about you and it is not even about the business; this is about helping your customer. You are not the most important element here, your customer is. It is not a personal critique on you and your business, it is about you doing what you already do well, better. It is about engaging with more customers to enable more customers to buy from you.

After all, you are in business in order to grow your business and the way to do this is to serve your customer better. Feedback and free information are to be welcomed; they are an invaluable, priceless, precious gift.

This is why I say that a complaint should be embraced with open arms. If you have one person complain, possibly ten others have walked away and have not complained but sadly will probably never use your business again.

Fill the gaps in your business

You want to know where those gaps are in your business so that you can start to fill them, you do not want another ten or even a hundred customers walking away who have not told you of the gap in standards. It is so important to embrace these opportunities; ignorance is not an excuse. It is so much better to hear from someone who had the courage to give feedback – thank them for giving the gift of feedback.

That gap in your business is losing you customers, and now you can fill that gap, improve your business and win more customers. Always think, "If I do this better I am going to win more custom".

Be brave enough to tell customers that you have corrected a mistake as a result of customer feedback. Thank the customer publicly. Customers look at you and your business and appreciate your honesty and transparency; it becomes the kind of business they would want to associate with. You can always turn negatives into positives if you are proactive.

Taking customer feedback on board creates a cycle of making little improvements in your business; absolutely brag about those improvements, and invite people to come in and help you to improve it even further. Furthermore, publicly celebrate your successes. This is beneficial for your employees, your customers, and you.

Maslow Hierarchy of Customer Service[20]

When we look at Maslow's hierarchy of customer service, as defined by Chip Conley, we see the triangle has three levels.

Level one: SURVIVAL

The bottom level is about SURVIVAL, just meeting your customer expectations and creating satisfaction. Most businesses are at this first level; some businesses are far below this level. We often hear in the media[21] that businesses in the UK are bad at customer service. Many UK businesses are only just meeting their customers' expectations and creating a low level of satisfaction. Customers have a very reactive perspective, they respond to the perspective that the business has of them. It comes down to whether, when a customer enquires or complains, their needs are met or the problem is solved satisfactorily. This is the base level of the customer satisfaction hierarchy of needs.

I, personally, am not happy with that level of service. I want to be more than satisfied – I want to be exhilarated, I want to be "wowed"! Many customers, however, are happy with the transactional, satisfactory level of service in the main – that is what they expect. Businesses are lucky if this is all customers are looking for. The sad thing is when businesses cannot even meet their customers at this low level.

Now, with social media, the rapid flow of information and easy access to global products and services, and enormous choice, customers are gaining power and raising their expectations. Businesses can no longer rest on their laurels; they must raise their standards of customer service and engagement and move up from the survival level.

Level two: DESIRES

Level two of the triangle is about understanding and fulfilling your customers' DESIRES: their pleasures. There are companies that are constantly gathering data from their customers, to analyse their habits and behaviours. Store cards gather data about how many times we buy, how much we spend, precisely what we purchase. These stores are constantly endeavouring to understand their customers.

*Amazon is brilliant at this: we buy something from Amazon and then they make suggestions of other things that are similar. They are taking the data that we provide and using the information to suggest other things we might like. We probably do not **need** the recommended products because we did not go looking for them but they may be things we **want**. Amazon feeds our desires.*

Amazon's customer service is at the higher level of understanding and fulfilling our desires. This is where the pleasure principle comes in: they are meeting the customers' needs but they are also speaking to their wants and desires.

This is a more proactive approach, taking data that the business collects internally or externally, analysing the information to coming up with solutions to meet customers' desires. It is possible to use modelling software and analytical tools to gather this data and analyse it but if you are a small business, the best method is to ask your customer-facing employees. The ones who speak to your customers, whether on the telephone or face-to-face. A customer-facing employee will have a very good idea of what your customers are looking for or, if they don't already know, they have the ability to ask the customer.

The second level of the hierarchy of customer service understands and fulfils your customers' desires. It is about standing in the shoes of your customers and looking at your business from the customers' perspective. Businesses will look at the data they have gathered through competitions and through other marketing strategies to understand the customer relationships and use the information to create loyal customers.

There are few organisations that consistently operate this strategy successfully. Many are trying to take customer data and use it intelligently, increase engagement and being proactive with the data to make the information beneficial to their customer.

Level three: TRANSFORMATIONAL

Level three is TRANSFORMATIONAL. It is not just meeting your customers' desires and creating loyalty because you understand your customers better, it is about anticipating and meeting their unrecognised desires and needs. This level is about creating an almost evangelical customer-base that absolutely loves what you do for them, they love who you are because you completely get them! Your product or service completes your customers' perceptions of their wants and desires. There are very few companies that operate at this transformational level.

Transformation is a wonderful thing because it is leaning in, and having a listening ear. It is the optimum level of, "What is your pleasure, Sir?" More – "I know, I even feel, your desires"! Transformation is all about the customer and very little about the business. The business is intuitive and knows what its customers' highest desires are. The business only exists for the customers' pleasure and therefore makes intelligent and clever connections about the customers' emotional experience. It is not a transaction; it is a holistic experience. It is looking at the total experience the customer will gain during the business journey, including their perception of what the business means. The business tunes-in and uses knowledge, experience and intuition to build the relationship up to a higher level of anticipated desire.

The business actively partners with its customers, has regular exchanges of information, conversations and interactions. The business and the customer experience is symbiotic/synergetic. This level entails not just standing in your customer's shoes, but being in your customer's head and heart. It is not just speaking the customer's language; it is finishing their sentences. The customer recognises this and "like attracts like". They absolutely love you because you are in their head. Customers feel that "you get them": you are completely in-tune with them. You are the brand imagined in their dreams.

Examples of the different levels

Level one: survival

At the survival level, I flew to America in May 2010 on United Airlines. Coming back to the UK we were delayed due to a volcanic ash cloud so United flew us to Canada. We got off the plane and waited for eight hours before eventually being told there would be no more flights until the next morning. United's message was to sort ourselves out or sleep at the airport.

Many planes had been diverted by that time so the airport was absolutely heaving. We had waited around for most of the day, so it was a complete and utter free-for-all. Customers were left to find their own transport, to ring hotels and to ring a customer service number of the airline to rebook their own flight home.

You can imagine the number of people who were trying to get through on this line, using the airport credit card phones, at premium rates. I managed to get a room at a beautiful hotel; it was a shame I couldn't enjoy the experience! In the hotel room I tried dialling the flight booking number from 11 pm; I redialled the engaged customer service number constantly and finally got through at 3 am and booked myself on a 7 am flight to the UK. I had two hours' sleep before making my way back to the airport for my flight home.

How ridiculous was it to have no support or help from the airline? Their view was that it was not their problem: the weather condition was outside their control; their only responsibility was to take us from 'A' to 'B'. Everything else in between was entirely up to us to organise; they were not interested in anything else. This is an example of a very low level of transactional customer service.

Level two: desire

When looking for an example of a level two business, which understands and fulfils customer desires, Virgin Atlantic fits this bill. They embrace social media to help build and engage a solid customer fan-base and to continually win over their customers to become fans. They use Twitter and Facebook to keep customers informed about flight cancellations, delays and weather problems. They are constantly listening and responding to their customers and they actively welcome complaints.

They are constantly communicating and that communication is informative, humorous and engaging.

When they make mistakes they are honest about them and they reimburse customers for delays. They are very open in their communications, sharing good news stories, like lost luggage being found. With their use of traditional and social media, even people who are not using Virgin services will engage with the business. Virgin is good at using the right messaging on a variety of platforms for their different customer segments, whether business or leisure customers.

Virgin managers are very clever in the way they understand their customers, the way they fulfil their customers' desires. Not only that, but they create desires within their customers through competitions, through their linked businesses and activities such as the V-festival, Virgin Pioneers and Virgin Media, each service appealing to different customer segments, each segment drawing new customers into the Virgin community, adding to the knowledge-bank and the service experience. Virgin is a great example of level two in building loyalty and meeting their customers' wants and desires.

Level three: transformational

An example of a level three, transformational business is Apple, guided by its founder, Steve Jobs. He was the epitome of someone who was an instinctive leader at the helm of a transformational business. Apple not only transformed the industry but transformed the user experience and expectations.

Under Steve Jobs, Apple was firmly at level three. He instinctively understood his customer base because he designed for himself; he was his own ideal customer. He created a massive fan base, an evangelical following, which still exists after his passing. Apple fans love the values and philosophy of Steve Jobs, thinking nothing of sleeping outside an Apple store for days in order to get the latest Apple product. You can imagine a fraternity of followers in their 60s reminiscing about the Steve Jobs Apple experience.

"Appleites" are not just customers; they are evangelical fans. Jobs was totally in tune with his kind of customer, the kind of person who believes that design and usability were equal in importance, if not more important, than the technical specification of the equipment. At the time that other competing businesses were at level two, continuing to create better technology for fixed computers, Steve Jobs popularised mobile technology.

Jobs was thinking what others were not and through Apple he transformed fixed and functional computers into movable Apples with a lifestyle brand. In so doing, Apple transformed the industry and transformed customers into evangelical fans. At a whole different level, in a technological industry his engagement was based on usability and design, not merely technology.

Steve Jobs was an example of a transformational leader leading a transformational business to create evangelical fans. This is the top level in the hierarchy of customer service.

What should you aim for?

If you are a level two business, brilliant! As a micro to medium businesses you can get to level two quicker if you can identify a clear customer profile, develop a close relationship, communicate intelligently with your customers and gain feedback which you act upon to transform the business and your relationships with your customers.

Where micro to medium businesses tend to fall down is capturing and analysing that data into useable information. But remember, you do not have to have all the analytical tools, you just need to have a process for collecting data, like asking your customer-facing employees and using the feedback and assimilating it into knowledge. Empower your employees to use their initiative to continually engage with your customers.

If you are a micro to medium business, this is easy to do. You do not need endless resources; you just need to empower your people. If you put this at a level of importance in your business strategy, it is easier to get to success level two in the hierarchy of customer service.

Level three is more difficult to attain but it is not impossible. If you have a niche or unique product or business you also have a point of difference to develop evangelical fans. If you are so engaged that you can almost finish the sentences of your customers, if you can fully anticipate what your customers' desires are and are able to give them what they desire, deliver on that promise, then you are at or approaching a level three, transformational business. As a level three business, to a certain extent you do not need to worry about the customer and the business in the same way as level one or two businesses. As the dynamics change, your problem becomes staying ahead and keeping your fans evangelical. You have now created a model for others to follow, so you have to move the model on before others catch up and even out-perform, as in the case of Apple and Samsung.

Your customers and evangelical fans are your best sales department. It is vital that you remain loyal to them and true to your brand. All you need to do is stay focused and two steps ahead. I am not saying you do not worry about the operations or finances but that will flow if the business is managed well. Word will spread like wildfire. What is critical is to recognise the importance and the magnitude of your customer relationships. Drill down on who your customers are. What are their desires? What is their pleasure?

Initially, answering these questions will involve proactively engaging and connecting with customers. Then you will start to have a dialogue with them, understand and anticipate their desires. Finally, you need to get closer to your most engaged customers, thus intuitively creating fans.

That is the ultimate place you want to be in business, instinctively knowing the answer before you ask the question, "What is your pleasure, Sir?"

Chapter six
Process

Almost all quality improvement comes via simplification of design, manufacturing ... layout, processes, and procedures.

Tom Peters

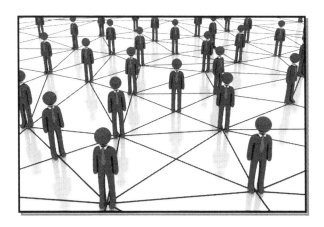

Aligning your processes to your customers' wants and desires

Alignment of the business processes relates to the operational processes within your business. It is also about aligning your products and services to your customers' wants and needs. Your customers get what they want, when they want it and how they want it. This is not about you: it is all about your customers, serving customers' needs and solving their problems.

This does not mean that you are a slave to the whims of your customer. It does not mean that the customer is always right. What alignment enables you to do is calculate the limits of your business's operational processes so you understand what you can deliver consistently well. Understanding your capabilities allows you to look at how you can maximise your resources. Once you understand that, you can offer your customers the products and services that will consistently solve their problems and meet their needs.

In the previous chapter we talked about the customers' pleasure, their desires, their wants, their needs and their pains; and also the messages you might use to motivate the customers to say, "I want that". This chapter is about your business fulfilling on that promise. It is your business getting the product or service to the customer in the most efficient way; the process is very streamlined – you are removing all of the barriers to your customer getting the promise, once they have said, "I want it".

Operations management

"Operations management is the overseeing, designing and controlling of the 'processes' of the production of your products or services."[22] It is your responsibility as a business owner or manager to ensure that the operation works efficiently, that you have the systems in place, the people in place so that you are delivering on the promise to the customers' requirements. You are looking at the processes, the activities, to get the customer what they want and desire.

The journey from concept to processes

As an entrepreneur, you create the business concept, you bring it to life and spend many hours nurturing it. You get it to a point where you have a few customers and you grow that customer base; everything is going well. As growth continues, you may need more support in your business. So you might get someone in the back office or a customer-facing role to help you deliver more product to the customer. You need to produce more processes and have more systems in place so that you can consistently get that product or service from 'A' to 'B'.

Depending on your business model, your product or service, 'A' could be creating awareness of your product or the customer saying, "I want that" and 'B' might be the customer actually enjoying the product. All of the activities that must happen to deliver 'A to B' are your sequenced processes that sit within the system. As the business grows, so do the number of processes and the systems become more complicated.

As your business grows, your role within the business moves from owner to manager. As a manager, you create processes to manage the resources (people and systems) and you have less direct contact with your customers. That is just a by-product of a business growing. You want your business to get bigger, you want to cater to more customer needs and you want to do what you do better.

The by-product of this is that you, as an entrepreneur and business owner, start to move further away from your customer. You have less day-to-day contact and fewer conversations with your customers, and you start managing the systems and the employees, creating barriers between you and your customer. Then because you move further away from the customer, you become a little distant. You enjoy the activity of the business: as it is growing you see more money coming in or more products going out. That is great, it is very rewarding.

What happens at this point, however, is that you may become very protective of the processes you have created, instead of being protective of the customer experience and the customer journey. Your relationship is now with the processes and the systems; the dynamics of the business move from being customer-focused to being business-focused and protective of the business itself.

It is very difficult for you to look at your business with fresh eyes and critique it from the customers' point-of-view. You typically lose connection with the customer and their point-of-view because you are so busy managing the resources of the business. You move so far away from your core purpose that you do not realise you are putting up barriers to the customers doing business with you, that the processes you are building create barriers.

What you should be trying to do is create a frictionless business. A frictionless business is one in which processes are intuitive and flow, one where there are no blockages or breaks in the processes. The idea is to make doing business simple and easy for your customer; to make the process seamless and fluid.

This brings down the costs of processing problems because problems will be few. It also reduces the transaction time so you can do more with less. The more resources you have to have in place to answer queries and resolve problems, the more it costs the business and the more it distracts you from your core purpose, the more you frustrate your customers, the fewer customers you will have and the harder it is to win them back if they leave.

What you want is for your processes to flow so you have more products going out to happy customers. You want an increase in the "doing" activities (creating and delivering your products and services) and a reduction in the "not-doing" activities, the areas that cost you money to resolve the problems of the processes in poorly designed and ill thought-out systems.

A frictionless business is a business customers come back to again and again. The biggest compliment a customer can give you is, "That was easy". That means you are creating a frictionless business, a simple business that flows.

Examples of businesses that are not in flow

We have all experienced businesses that are not in flow. Most of us have experienced this with call centres. We feel frustration when we hear people reading scripts. We simply want to speak to someone who is going to solve our problem now. How hard can that be? Call centres create barriers because you have to follow their linear process. It can feel like call centre workers are the gatekeepers, deliberately creating barriers to reduce their company's cost of service and frustrating their customers in the process.

Customers are not linear and they do not want robotic processes. Customers want personality and colour. Human character and connection create pleasurable experiences. When I hear a script I feel like a product on an assembly line. Call centres in general are designed for the benefit of the company and not the customer.

There is a way of creating a service that customers enjoy interacting with, where problems are resolved and customers feel a human connection. Examples of this are below. It might cost businesses more up-front but if it engages and creates happy customers and enhances the brand rather than eroding it, the additional cost might be worth the increased value.

Here is a personal example of processes getting in the way of my experience as a customer. I went to the theatre having booked online (that part was fairly straightforward) but when I turned up at the box office there was a long queue and there were only two people serving. The theatre box office was clearly short-staffed, the staff were under pressure and apologetic.

As there was only one queue, it did not matter whether you were just picking up pre-paid tickets or you were buying tickets and choosing your seats. The servers would have processed many more people had they separated the fast and slow transactions into two queues. Had the servers separated the queue they might have realised that 85% of the queuing customers were fast pre-paid pick-ups and that the purchasing customers could wait. The queue would move faster, most of the customers would not be as frustrated and the servers not as defeated by the waiting crowd.

As I waited, I could see through the box office into the bar, where there were three people serving drinks and no queue. I was dying for a drink but like many others I couldn't get to the bar because I was in the box office queue. As I got towards the front of the queue my friends arrived and the auditorium bell sounded, I collected my tickets and we just had enough time to go straight into the auditorium to be seated. There was no time for pre-theatre drinks or to order drinks for the intermission.

During the intermission we sat in the auditorium talking and did not go to the bar. The theatre lost money because I couldn't buy a drink at the beginning of the evening and couldn't be bothered to join another busy queue to buy a drink in the intermission. There may have been hundreds of customers of the same mind – that is a lot of revenue to be losing on a daily basis. The inefficient box office processes created a poor customer experience (I was dehydrated, irritated and could not remember the performance) plus a loss of revenue.

Misdirected resources

I often see resources being utilised in the wrong place at the wrong time. What we require are multi-skilled employees who have the authority to allocate themselves where needed and a clear vision, systems and processes to support the business they are in, which is perhaps "giving customer joy". This requires an independent spirit. Business resources need to be dynamic in reacting to customer needs.

Customers have on average only a fifteen minute window of tolerance to use the theatre facilities; if this business has not given joy outside the auditorium it will affect the experience inside.

As customers we get used to poor service, but from a business point of view you need to look at the barriers you erect that prevent your customers doing business with you. Look at your processes from your customers' perspective. Are you making it easy or hard? Is it simple and intuitive or difficult and counterintuitive?

There is evidence that the time wasted in British businesses is mostly due to excess bureaucracy. The staff on the bar probably knew that they should help in the box office, but had likely not been given the authority to use their common sense. There is a phenomenon called "cultural inertia"[23] where employees will not take the initiative because a strong or hierarchical culture stifles a dynamic environment.

The culture of an organisation may be one where if, "My manager has not told me" to do something, it doesn't get done. It is important to adopt the right type of culture for the business to consistently achieve the desires of its customers. It is essential that customer-facing employees be empowered to use their common sense to do what is right for the customer. Business is not just about you creating the right processes; it is about you also creating the right culture.

Seven per cent of employees in customer-facing businesses say sales opportunities are missed as a result of the poor systems that are in place.[24] This results in 16% customer dissatisfaction.[25] Additionally, in some industries, poor systems may account for 30% loss of business.[26] Streamlining systems means you can make more money in your business with little or no cost implication.

How to recognise processes that are not working

My process motto is: "If it is not flowing it is not going". There are always clear indications where there are blocks in your business. Here's another example.

I went to Wimbledon and attempted to buy a cup of coffee and a piece of cake. It took me over fifteen minutes of queuing to get them and by then I was very frustrated with the process. It is a matter of process alignment. The stewards in the grounds at Wimbledon were exemplary in the way they directed the spectators, the processes were simple and the resources were moved to the crunch points, right time, right place. In contrast, the food and drink operation was poorly devised and executed.

The sandwiches and cakes were self-service but hot drinks had to be ordered. There was a queue for cappuccinos and another express queue for black coffee. No one knew what the sign "express" meant. Most of the customers were in the wrong queue, which created huddles and blockages. Then once you got to the front of the queue and got your coffee, you had to then join another queue for the cash tills. I had been waiting five minutes in the queue for my coffee, so why couldn't I have paid for everything I had then?

When you mix self-service with pre-ordering facilities, particularly in small units, it is very difficult for customers to flow. Customers will pick up some of what they want and then they have to order and wait for something which stops the flow. Mixing the two didn't work, it was a disaster, there was no flow.

It was so disappointing, especially as the customer experience at the gate and in the ground is excellent. The coffee was in a tiny cup and tasted like wet water. It took longer to buy than it did to drink. My experience was so poor that in a ten hour day I only went to the café twice. As for many leisure and entertainment businesses, the food and drink operations are crucial to the profitability of the business.

My friends wonder why I am impatient; they are so used to putting up with poor service, poor processes and poor operations that they do not see that is it poor. It is their norm.

Embrace complaints

I want more customers to ask more of businesses and to complain more often when they don't get satisfaction. And I want more businesses to embrace customer complaints and to deliver better, more targeted services to WOW their customers.

A good way of recognising there is something wrong with the process is when queues are not moving, when you have customers who look directionless or huddles of people but no queue is forming. If you have given people a line and there is a sign giving clear instructions, customers usually follow it! So design your facility to help your customers to understand the process. Then you will not have huddles of frustrated customers. People get frustrated when simple, regular activities are made difficult for them or they do not know what is going on. A little communication would resolve the issue; make it easy for your customer.

Surprisingly, I have seen poor process management at many of the big coffee chains. They should make coffee in the sequence that customers order, yet so often I see staff crossing over one another, I see a lack of communication and a lack of attention with dirty cups sitting on dirty tables. There is little teamwork and communication so the system works well when the shop is not busy but confusion persists when it is.

Disgruntled customers are another sign of poor process. I complain often. I recently said to an assistant in a coffee shop, "as interesting as your conversation is, I have been standing here waiting for my coffee to be served and it's been sitting on the machine crying out for your attention". The assistant thought I was rude, but I thought after five minutes of standing in front of them listening to their conversation that I was being remarkably polite.

I must add that I have started up and run a restaurant and bar which was awarded for its service standards, therefore my expectations of other businesses in this sector are realistic. I want to feel and know the business cares about their customers; attention is evidence of this.

Businesses are well-advised to embrace irritants like me, to discover more about the problem so they can resolve it quickly. You should take people like me to your manager because I will tell them how to fix the broken processes. People like me are a valuable resource. We test your processes and highlight the blocks and gaps and we can become your best advocates if handled well. We tell you how to improve and possibly grow, and the added bonus is that all our critiques are free!

Complaints are fantastic. There will be many customers who will get fed up but won't complain. The customers who complain give you valuable information. You can interrogate them, learn more and see it from their perspective. That makes it a lot easier for you to resolve problems and improve your processes.

Align your processes to your customers' needs

Talk to your customers and align your processes to their needs. You cannot afford to lose customers; you cannot afford to have frustrated customers. You cannot afford for their money and custom to be walking out of your door.

If customers are hitting your website and leaving again because they cannot find what they want, because they cannot understand what you do or your payment system is too long-winded – or kicks them out so that they have to start again – for you that is lost income, lost business and lost revenue. Customers will only try a few times and if it is difficult then they will not buy at all; at least not from you. You cannot afford to waste money, to lose customers, or to have your employees constantly resolving problems rather than serving more customers

Costs increase when processes are inefficient

Many businesses are not aware that their processes are not working for their customers and so are not conscious of how much poor processing is costing them.

If you can get a member of staff to tell you how much of their day is taken up resolving problems, then work that out in a salary, it will motivate you to resolve some of these blocks in your processes. Often it is the same problem happening over and over again, so you only have to resolve that problem in your system and processes once.

It is so simple that it makes me wonder why entrepreneurs and business owners do not look into their processes. Why waste money in your business? You do not have money to waste and you do not have customers to lose! Flowing processes are powerful and profitable.

As I mentioned before, take a customer journey through your business or go to a similar business and look at it with a very critical customer's eye. Record the journey in a flow chart, moving your customer from 'A' to 'B'. Note all of the interactions, all of the touch points in between, to get them to the point of enjoying the product. Then look at where you can make the savings; that is saving time and simplifying the process, not reducing the quality.

Exercise Thirteen: Create your ideal customer experience

List every touch point (interaction) in your customers' journey from 'A' to 'B'

Review each touch point where you can add value or clarity, cut out or streamline the process/activity. This should be done with all the employees who are involved in the processes giving suggestions for improvements.

Record your ideal customer experience journey and communicate it to all employees who engage in the process or interact with your customer.

Measure and monitor how often your business delivers the ideal customer experience.

Celebrate the successes of "wowing" your customers.

Look at how you can simplify your overall process and make it frictionless. How can you make it more succinct? How can you communicate to the customer the way the process works? How easy it is? Are there bits of that process you can bypass? Can you change the distribution channel so the customer doesn't have to come to you at all? Can you anticipate what the customer may need? If they have ordered a product and they order it on a regular basis, then rather than them having to keep ordering it, why not just send it to them? You could miss that bit out entirely by having a yearly agreement with them. It may be that you have saved them a day over the year by streamlining that process.

Plotting the journey allows you to understand the entire path so you can see where you can make savings, for yourself and for the customer.

Streamlined processes create loyalty

Sometimes when you make a change to the service to make it more beneficial to the customer — perhaps even turn it into a service they cannot get anywhere else — it saves you money as well. Is that not powerful? The customer thinks you are wonderful, to be doing all of this for them, but you are also helping yourself by helping your customer. It makes them loyal and it creates a barrier against competitors. If your business was to anticipate the needs of your customers, why would your customer go anywhere else?

Managing expectations

Let's go back to the physiotherapist I talked about earlier. A potential customer is in pain and they want immediate relief. If they call and get an answer-phone message saying, "I am in a consultation. I will call you back", what are they likely to do? They will probably put the phone down and ring the next number on the list. It is very frustrating for the customer when they cannot get to speak to someone when motivated by pain. It is the same when you are booking a doctor's appointment: you are in pain, you want relief and you want it now.

Have you ever made a call to a business, not getting through to the person you need and the receptionist asks you to call back later? I have, and wondered, why have a receptionist? The receptionist should take my number or put me through to an answer-phone, right? I think, "I have just called you, why should I call you again? Why should I keep calling you? I have already called you once, surely if you are the receptionist then you can take my details down and ask the receiver to call me back? Is that not declaring, 'You the customer are important to us, we want your custom, we want your information, and we want to keep you on board as a valued customer. We are going to call you because we do not want to lose you'?"

How often do you get in a situation where you have to keep calling back to get hold of somebody, or you leave a message on the answer-phone, or you send an email and it is three days before they come back, if at all? Even if it is just an acknowledgment saying, "I have your information, I am dealing with it", that would be preferable.

I am not in favour of automated messages saying, "I will come back to you in 24 hours", it is too impersonal, but at least it is some acknowledgement. Managing expectations is about having simple, effective communication processes to respond to customers in a timely manner.

The right level of communication

It is important, when you are communicating with your customers, that you take into account their preferences. I do not like to be bombarded with lots of communication. I like to request information when I want it, so I am very reluctant to sign up to a long trail of information.

There are other people who like that regular information. Some people like information via email and some like telephone conversations. You need to find out what customers you have and you need to meet them where they are, rather than expecting them to meet you. Not all customers are equal, so do not treat them as such. Your processes need to meet your customers' varying expectations.

The only way to do that is to ask the customer how often they want to hear from you. Ask them how they want you to respond. Is it via email or telephone? If they say by telephone, do not email them. Make sure that if you are going to collect data from customers that you do not frustrate them by ignoring it.

Make sure you manage their expectations. Ask them what their expectations are and put the processes in place to meet them and offer a variety of access points: telephone, email, social media, website contact etc.

More customers for the physiotherapist

A physiotherapist is in the business of pain relief. The important point is that their potential customers want immediate pain relief. They do not want to get an answer-phone message, they want to get hold of someone right away. After reviewing all the options and the business processes, we employed a receptionist. Of course, this cost the company more money but in the long run it brought in far more money that it cost.

We also put a much more visible sign up outside the premises with the words, "Pain Relief Here. Emergency Appointments Available", with an arrow pointing to where people could park off the busy road.

The physio's diary was scheduled so that every two hours there was a half an hour slot free for emergency appointments. That meant that normally no one had to wait more than an hour to have a consultation; and because the diary was spaced to accommodate walk-ins, the messaging around the advertising basically said, "We encourage emergencies and walk-ins".

The receptionist was available so that customers received personal and immediate contact – and the receptionist could make sure that those in pain were looked after and given lots of reassurance. A one hour wait, when you are in pain, feels like eternity; to have somebody there looking after your customers, to offer a glass of water or a cup of tea, or distract with conversation, can make a big difference.

The receptionist would also ring new customers to ask how there were feeling post-treatment, and to inform them that although they were booked in for another appointment, if anything happened in the interim they should call and they *would be fitted in for another emergency appointment. So it is not just that appointment, it is the pre- and post-care as well.*

Regular visitors, for instance, received follow-up calls if their x-rays arrived and reminders to book another appointment. It was building personal relationships: the receptionist knew the customers by name. The receptionist also reminded customers of their appointments by email or telephone message or SMS. Customers were asked how they wanted to receive this information to make sure the process worked for them. The reminders reduced missed appointments by 60% because many customers book appointments weeks in advance and then forget them. Customers were encouraged to call if running late, so waiting customers' times and customer expectations are managed: everyone is more relaxed and happy.

The business also got more referrals because the receptionist would talk to the customers, find out about their families and their backgrounds and if there was a family member or friend who was also experiencing pain. The receptionist would then say, "Ask X to come along and we will fit them in", and in this way customers were given subtle messages about referring more people to the practice.

The new processes worked by bringing in new customers through scheduling the diary for emergency appointments, and by employing and training a receptionist who practised pain management and aftercare and worked with the existing customer base, especially encouraging them to refer more people. With time the receptionist managed the stock, increased sales of products and did the book-keeping. New processes completely turned around this business.

Improve the design of your processes

Every business owner is different, every business is different, every customer segment is different, the geography, the location, it is all different, so as I give examples, look for nuggets in all business sectors.

Working with a high street retailer (a pharmacy) their customers had difficulty finding anything in the store. It was like the signs on the aisles were in another language; it was just difficult to find your way around.

Lots of businesses lay out their products in a way that makes sense to the business – because it is easy for stock-taking or it reduces the amount of stealing from the shelves, or they have designed the shop to be beautiful, forgetting the customer experience. Whatever the reason, it is completely illogical to the customer. It is easy for the business, but often these things have no rhyme or reason to the customer.

This retailer had so many different products that it was confusing the customers. You could never get the attention of the busy assistants, who spent all their time directing customers. The employees and customers were surveyed to get their views and learn about their frustrations then suggested solutions, substantive/transformative changes were made.

We categorised the store by symptoms with overhead signs saying "colds" or "dental". Customers could go into the store, look up and go to the relevant section. If the customer had a toothache or a headache, they could just look up and a sign would point them to the right section.

Then we reduced their stock to have fewer variations on the theme. For example, how does a customer choose between three time release, three drowsy and three non-drowsy headache packets? It is costly for small pharmacies to hold large stock, which ties up cash-flow and customers get confused by too many options. I am intelligent enough to know whether drowsy or non-drowsy suits my requirements: in the night time I might take drowsy and during the day I want non-drowsy; I might prefer time-release, I might prefer the bigger tablets, I might prefer the effervescent ones – but the greater the number of options the more difficult the decision. Having several products that do the same thing is confusing to the customer. If there is one product that does a specific thing, it makes it easy for the customer to choose.

Labelling of the aisles enabled the customer to walk around, and think, "I want some toothpaste as well" because they can see the section above their head as they walk out towards the cash till. Customers go in for one thing and walk out with five different things because finding their way around the store is very easy. Also it is quick and easy to make decisions with fewer options of the right product.

Now the customers are self-sufficient because the signage leads the customer round to the right section, which means the businesses can have more staff on the tills and fewer on the floor helping to direct customers; this reduces queues and customers' waiting time; the business flows better.

Profits increased by more than 50%.

Think about what you need to do in your business to maximise your operational processes and improve the design. You need to look at how people flow, where you want them to walk around the store. Where are the cash tills? Are they dotted around your business or all at one point? Whichever it is, there has got to be a reason that makes sense so that customers understand and flow easily.

Is the signage in your business directing customers to the right place so they can make a decision? Is the stock you have in your business complicated or simple? Is the ticketing and labelling for the products simple? Does the product have pricing on it? Do you have pricing per kilo so that people can do a comparison between similar products to work out which is good value? Do you offer a value and a premium level of service? Are your processes simple and clear to the customer?

These are the things you need to think about, things you need to make easy for your customer. If processes are easy, the customer experience is better, they will be able to buy quicker, flow through quicker and they will probably buy more from you. It is important to look at those things in your business.

Customer feedback is brilliant

You might think customer feedback is bad but it is actually brilliant, it is what you need! Make sure at every touch point in your business (whether online or customer-facing) that you gather some information from the customer. Not just whether they have enjoyed the experience but what they enjoyed about it. What aspect of the service made them the happiest? Is there anything they would want you to improve upon? You want to do more of the thing that makes customers happy.

Get feedback from your customers. Are they complaining and angry? Great! You have got past the British politeness and you are going to get valuable information out of them.

Look at how customers flow around your business, how your website is designed, where your customers go online, how they move around the physical operation of the business. Is your business designed to allow your customers to flow intuitively?

Keeping customers engaged

My message here is simple: appeal to your customers and engage with them. You may want to offer them little incentives to give you more information. If it is a particular customer segment you want more from, create offers and incentives that get them to answer questions and give information so you can better serve their wants and needs. Ensure they win something they want. It is about giving more to get more.

You need to give the customer what they want, how they want it and when they want it, and you need to do it consistently within the limitations of your business resources; the only way to do that is to ask them.

Give the customer what they want

I will give you a fantastic example: Koreans are the hardest working group of people in the world[27] and so time is very precious to them. The number one retailer in Korea is a supermarket chain.

Then Tesco entered the Korean market wanting to be the number one supermarket retailer. They looked at the particular customer character and culture, to get to know their customer wants and needs, their behaviours, their pleasures and their pains. They got close to the customer, discovered they are the hardest working people and their time is limited, so any supermarket shopping trip cost Koreans precious time.

Thus Tesco designed a whole new way of shopping. Koreans embrace mobile technology. South Korea is one of the most advanced digital nations in the world, ranking third in the world for transaction motivated interactions.[28] Tesco created "virtual" stores.[29] Within metro subway transport stations, they rolled out pictures of fully stocked aisles, so as commuters walked through the subway on their way to work, they would see pictures of aisles set out like a supermarket store. Then they would use their smartphone to scan the QR-code and this would create an order. People would go round this virtual store scanning the products that they wanted and by the time they got home their order would have been delivered.

It meant Tesco did not have to spend money to compete for space, building more supermarkets that Koreans did not enjoy going to anyway. They were already travelling though the subway on their way to or from work, and most of them had smartphones. What a brilliant, frictionless business idea! It made it easy for customers to transact on the go.

Tesco streamlined the processes and brought the supermarket to the customers, so the customers could do their shopping while they were en-route, with their purchases simply delivered to their home. It is a frictionless process! This is a fantastic business model. It is cost-effective and works for the benefit of the customer!

Think about how you could do this in your business: streamline your processes and make it simple and easy for both your customer and your business; re-engineer the processes so that yours becomes a frictionless business. Remove all the barriers for your customer doing business with you. Design your business around your customers. Do not expect your customer to adapt to your business processes.

Once the customer starts ordering in this easy way at the subway station, do you think they are going to go back to the old traditional supermarket queues? If they can get everything through this easy process do you think they are going to move back to an experience that they do not enjoy and which costs them more of their valuable time? Of course they are not.

That frictionless business has essentially made customers for life. All Tesco needs to do is keep improving on that new model, adding value so the new way of shopping becomes the norm. This is absolutely brilliant!

Other examples of this are Amazon and eBay. I do not have to put in my credit card details whenever I want to buy something. I might be buying items from a whole host of different stores, operators and suppliers, but because I am transacting through eBay, all I have to do is click to pay. eBay has my payment details, delivery address, etc saved; it is a frictionless payment system. It is also simpler for each supplier as they don't have to collect the payment themselves.

Start to think about how you can make yours a seamless, frictionless business. It reduces the cost of you doing business and also makes it easier for the customer – and customers will buy more from you because it is so easy.

"Wow" the customer

I absolutely love "wowing" my customers. We talked in the Pleasure chapter about transformational businesses and I gave Apple as an example. "Wowing" follows on from this. It is not just collecting data and churning it back out, but being intuitive about your customers' desires and going above and beyond their expectations. How can you extend your service to partner your customer? What more can you do to anticipate what their desires are? Could you lead their aspirations? Let me give you an example:

A workman did some work in the home of a family. It was a relatively small job but it is very personal working in the family environment, knowing the family dynamics, even the name of the dog. He returned the next day to collect final payment.

When the workman arrived in the morning he brought breakfast for the whole family: croissants, muffins and fruit salad, and drinks from the coffee shop. He arrived when he knew the family would be getting ready before school and work. It was such a wonderful thing, an unexpected gesture and the family enjoyed a special breakfast. Everyone was happy and even the children enjoyed the experience. The parents were completely gobsmacked. It probably cost £20 to buy breakfast, less than 1% of the value of the job. That was a small price to pay for the returns it brought. The remaining payment was handed over and the workman left the customer and family to enjoy their breakfast.

For ages the parents talked about that experience to their family, friends and colleagues. They spread the word. The workman got so much referred business because the parents became real advocates for his business. Other family members, work colleagues and friends booked him – and all for the price of breakfast!

"Wowing" does not have to cost much money; it is about thinking ahead and planning. How can you give your customer what they want, when they want it, how they want it and more? How can you anticipate what will work for your customer? What worked for that family unit might not work for a different family unit; it is about being engaged with your customers' aspirations and lifestyles so that your business can consistently deliver and exceed expectations. How can you go above and beyond? What is meaningful and relevant for your customer, not you and your business?

Another simple example is the selling of products online and/or sending products through the post: to impress customers you can offer tracking facilities so that they know where the product is and when it will be delivered. A few days later you might ring the customer and say, "I believe the product arrived on this day, I just want to make sure that it arrived safely and intact. Have you put it up? If you need any support in doing this, here is the number to call, and we will talk you through it." It only takes one minute to leave a message which shows you care, and it creates an impression which lasts.

"Wowing" is about taking extra care. You take that extra care at the point when the product is there. You take it in the way the customer likes to receive that information (by telephone, text message or email) and you take it at the time when the customer is not busy (maybe in their lunch hour or after work, not when they are in the middle of family time). To "wow" you need to find out a little bit about the customer, or the type of customer, that you are dealing with. Customers love a bit of aftercare. So few businesses do this nowadays – make your service different and irresistible, show you take care.

Many businesses these days do not even give basic standards of service. They do not meet customers' basic expectations. To get an aftercare service is something that is very simple but it can absolutely "wow" your customer because it creates 'Raving Fans'[30]. So few businesses do it well. These become people who are completely awe-stuck with your service. What can you do so your customers are awe-struck? What can you do to transform your business and culture to create more raving fans, more awe-struck customers?

Your vision for an ideal customer experience

Look at the vision you want to create of your ideal customer experience. For this, you have to understand what your customer experience is. Go back to mapping out the processes that take your customers from 'A' to 'B'. You need to understand that each touch point is an opportunity. Ensure doing business with you gives customers a great customer experience. Make your process as streamlined as possible. What is the optimum customer experience you will be able to offer your customers? Your answer must be one you can consistently offer within the limits of your limited resources.

From the previous chapters you understand who your ideal customer is and the optimal experience you would like to give them. Once you have understood this, there needs to be a focus in your business on making the optimal customer experience a reality. What do you need to do to make that happen? Do you need a budget for buying breakfast? Do you need to have somebody to do the after care, someone who mans the phone or sends an email at 7 pm?

You might need to put those processes, those people, those resources in place to make "wow" happen. It is not going to happen on its own; but you can create the right environment for this to happen. Put the plan in place and grow towards it in small, deliberate steps. There may be a whole host of things you could do, but just start with one thing, do it well and do it consistently. Then move on to the next step in your plan to "wow" your customer and do it well and do it consistently.

Evolving your business

Do not try and eat the elephant whole, just chew it one bite at a time. You have got to have the vision, the aspiration in place to "wow" your customers. You have got to have the vision and plan to create raving fans. You have got to have the commitment to create a transformational business. The start of all this is that you have got to get closer to your customers and understand your customers' pleasure (wants and needs). You need clear focus on your values, your personality, what you do that no one else does, in the way that you do it and have clarity about "what business you are in".

Putting your personality into your business allows your customers to identify and engage with you. You differentiate yourself and your business, you get to know your customers, you streamline your processes and you align your business to the needs, the desires — the pleasures – of your customers.

And in the process, your business will evolve and grow. The business world is changing rapidly. You need a new way of thinking about business and a new way of interacting with customers: be global, thinking local (niche) and acting personal.

A note from Janice

Congratulations on reading this book and taking the steps towards evolving your business. This is the start of your journey. I hope to have motivated your thinking into "immediate" and "positive" action. Business is dynamic, which is why I love it.

Review your exercises and notes, mull over (to embed not to procrastinate) the journey. Business Evolution will help you get clarity and plan your path to your business growth through the themes of Personality, Purpose, Pleasure and Process. This is your Business Evolution and it is you who will create growth in the rapidly changing world of business.

I would love to receive comment or feedback from you, my customers. You can contact me through my website www.theproblem-solver.co.uk The great thing about business evolution is that there is no wrong answer. This is your journey. There is a right answer, however, and that is when your customers say yes! ☺

Next steps

Other places to connect with me:

www.twitter.com/janicebg

uk.linkedin.com/in/janicebgordon

www.facebook.com/TheProblemSolver.jbg

Subscribe to my newsletter to receive information about publications and events: www.theproblem-solver.co.uk

Book Janice B Gordon the award winning business consultant and business mentor

View my transformational mentoring and mastermind online program: www.theproblem-solver.co.uk/online.html

Book Janice B Gordon for keynote speaking engagements www.janicebgordon.co.uk:
Please email info@theproblem-solver.co.uk

~~~~~~~~~~

If you have enjoyed

Business Evolution

Creating growth in the changing world of business

Please post your review on Amazon and connect with me at any of the addresses above

I welcome your feedback

With my very great thanks,

Janice.

References

[1] Mitchell, J Sr. Tac "35 awesome rare quotes that will kick you in the ass" Addicted 2 Success accessed 19th February 2014

<http://addicted2success.com/motivation/35-awesome-rare-quotes-that-will-get-kick-you-in-the-ass>

[2] Federation of Small Businesses October 2013, *Small Business Statistics,* Department for Business Innovation and Skills. accessed 1st October 2013 <www.fsb.org.uk/stats>

[3] Department for Business, Innovation & Skills 23 October 2013, *Number of private sector businesses surpasses last year's record high,* accessed 25th October 2013

<https://www.gov.uk/government/news/number-of-private-sector-businesses-surpasses-last-years-record-high>

Official figures show that the number of private sector businesses in the UK has reached 4.9 million, eclipsing the record levels of last year. The new record is down to an increase of 102,000 businesses. The 4.9 million businesses fall almost entirely in the small and medium-sized category, with businesses employing fewer than 250 people making up 99% of the total number.

Those employing fewer than 50 employees make up nearly half of all businesses and account for a third of private sector turnover.

[4] "Commission" Official Journal of the European Union, *Definition of micro, small and medium-sized enterprises adopted by the commission*, 6th May 2003, Recommendation by the European Commission 2003/361/EC dating from 060503, Annex Article 2, accessed 1st November 2013

<http://eur-lex.europa.eu/LexUriServ/LexUriServ.do?uri=OJ:L:2003:124:0036:0041:EN:PDF>

The European Union EU defines micro-enterprises as those that meet 2 of the following 3 criteria and have not failed to do so for at least 10 years:

- fewer than 10 employees
- balance sheet total below EUR 2 million
- turnover below EUR 2 million.

[5] Dr Seuss. (1959) *Happy Birthday to You* , Random House, New York

[6] Janice B Gordon 2013, accessed 10th August 2013 <http://www.janicebgordon.co.uk>

[7] Janice B Gordon 2013, accessed 10th August 2013 <http://www.theproblem-solver.co.uk>

[8] Byrne, D. *June 1997, An Overview (and Underview) of Research and Theory within the Attraction Paradigm* Academic Press. Journal of Social and Personal Relationships, *vol. 14 no. 3 417-431* quoted in

R. Matthew Montoya, *September 10, 2013, A Two-Dimensional Model for the Study of Interpersonal Attraction* Personality and Social Psychology *Review 0: 1088868313501887v1-1088868313501887* accessed 1st December 2013

<http://psr.sagepub.com/content/early/2013/08/30/1088868313501887>

[9] Ayaz Nanji, June 19, 2013 *How Running a Small Business Has Changed,* MarketingProfs accessed December 27th 2013 <http://www.marketingprofs.com/charts/2013/10990/how-running-small-business-has-changed-infographic#ixzz2ogj9x6f9> _

[10] Jenna Goudreau 26 April 2010, *What Men And Women Are Doing On Facebook,* Forbes, accessed 10th September 2013

<www.forbes.com/2010/04/26/popular-social-networking-sites-forbes-woman-time-facebook-twitter.html>

[11] Jan Johnson Wondra, 22 November 2010, *Marketing truth in a :10 world*, Examiner, quoting J Walker Smith Yankelovich Consumer Research, accessed 27th December 2013 <http://www.examiner.com/article/marketing-truth-a-10-world>

[12] Saul McLeod updated 2013, *Maslow's Hierarchy of Needs,* Simply Psychology

A. H. Maslow "A Theory of Human Motivation" (1943) accessed 10th August 2013

< http://www.simplypsychology.org/maslow.html>.

[13]Daniel Goleman, 2007, *Three Kinds of Empathy: Cognitive, Emotional, Compassionate,* Daniel Goleman, accessed 10th October 2013

<http://danielgoleman.info/three-kinds-of-empathy-cognitive-emotional-compassionate>. Daniel Goleman, internationally known psychologist and a science journalist Goleman reported on the brain and behavioural sciences for *The New York Times*, his 1995 book, *Emotional Intelligence* was on *The New York Times* bestseller list for over a year

[14] Janet Christie, September 2013 *Jo Malone on her fragrance empire and battling cancer*, Jo Malone on her fragrance empire and battling cancer, accessed 10th October 2013, <http://www.scotsman.com/lifestyle/jo-malone-on-her-fragrance-empire-and-battling-cancer-1-2936313>

[15] Owners Tom Barton and Phil Eles Honest Burger 2013, accessed 1st October 2013

<http://www.honestburgers.co.uk>

[16] Kendra Cherry 2013, *What is the ID*, About.comPsychology, accessed 27th December 2013 <http://psychology.about.com/od/iindex/g/def_id.htm>

[17] Mumsnet by parents for parents 2013, accessed 1st November 2013, <http://www.mumsnet.com>

[18] LinkedIn.com 2013, accessed 1st November 2013, https://uk.linkedin.com also Twitter.com 2013, https://twitter.com and Facebook.com 2013, https://www.facebook.com

[19]Campus Party 2013, Telefonica, accessed 1st November 2013<http://www.campus-party.eu/2013/index-cpeu.html> promoting digital skills in Europe

[20] Chip Conley 2007 Peak: How great companies get their mojo from Maslow, Jossey-Bass, USA, p. 103.

<http://www.amazon.com/Peak-Great-Companies-Their-Maslow/dp/0787988618>
Understand the motivations of employees, customers, bosses, and investors, and use that understanding to foster better relationships and build an enduring and profitable corporate culture.

[21] Ed Cumming 12th January 2011, *Why is British service so bad?* Telegraph accessed 1st 16th July 2013

<http://www.telegraph.co.uk/culture/8253472/Why-is-British-service-so-bad.html>. "There is a reluctance on the part of British staff to admit that they are serving, rather than simply passers-by doing the restaurateur, and by extension you the customer, some kind of unpleasant favour. Mostly this stems from our obsession with, and microscopic sensitivity to, class".

[22] The Institute of Operations Management 2013, *What is Operations management?* IOM, accessed 16th August 2013

<https://www.iomnet.org.uk/Home/WhatisOperationsManagement.aspx>. "Further, it involves the responsibility of ensuring that business operations are efficient in terms of using as few resources as needed, and effective in terms of meeting customer requirements. It is concerned with managing the process that converts inputs (in the form of materials, labour and energy) into outputs (in the form of goods and/or services)."

[23] Carrillo, Juan D. and Gromb, (October 2002), *Cultural Inertia and Uniformity in Organizations*, Journal of Law, Economics, & Organization, accessed 1st September 2013 <http://www-bcf.usc.edu/~juandc/PDFpapers/wp-cult.pdf>

[24] Computerworld UK, 27 February 09, *Poor business process management hurts quarter of staff,* accessed 26th August 2013, <http://bit.ly/OzFQr5>

[25] Ibid.

[26] Ibid

[27] Forbes 21st May 2008, *The World's Hardest-Working Countries,* accessed 1st November 2013

<http://www.forbes.com/2008/05/21/labor-market-workforce-lead-citizen-cx_po_0521countries.html>

[28] Ecommerce Week, Friday October 11 2013, *Are you Digitally Normal? : Study reveals what makes each country click*, Mindshare Digital Normalness Index (MDNI), accessed 10th December 2013,

http://www.ecommerceweek.co.uk/news/119/are-you-digitally-normal-:-study-reveals-what-makes-each-country-click

[29] Recklessnutter, n.d.,*Tesco Homeplus virtual subway store in South Korea*, accessed 20th June 2013, <http://www.youtube.com/user/Recklessnutter?feature=watch>

[30] Ken Blanchard, (May 19th 1993) Raving Fans: A Revolutionary Approach To Customer Service, William Morrow.

ABOUT THE AUTHOR

Janice B Gordon, also known as "The Problem Solver", helps businesses move forward and grow. She views the world of business in a unique way, instantly seeing paths through current circumstances and helping business owners gain new perspectives and chart their course to increased success.

Janice holds a BA (Hons) in Design and Business Studies and a post graduate diploma from the Chartered Institute of Marketing (CIM), as well as an Executive MBA from Cranfield School of Management. She is a visiting Fellow with Cranfield's Centre for Strategic Marketing and Sales,

---

delivering Key Account Management and customised client programmes and assisting companies develop leading edge capabilities in managing their customer relationships.

Janice has contracted for global organisations Cambridge University Press, BP, AOL, HSBC, has worked as head of operations for a construction business and a membership charity, and as an Independent Financial Advisor (IFA) with an accountancy practice advising micro to medium businesses.

She set up a design business with sales channels in Europe and the USA. Janice then branched out on her own to create an award-winning 5000 square foot restaurant and style bar, and over four years grew it to employ twenty staff; moving on from this, and utilising all the skills she has gained over her years in all aspects of business, she is now an award winning director of the consultancy, The Problem Solver, providing micro to medium businesses with bespoke growth strategies, customer relationships processes and transformational mentoring programmes.

Janice B. Gordon is passionate about every aspect of the world of business.

39057610R00131

Made in the USA
Charleston, SC
23 February 2015